CW01646093

My Menopause, My Way

How to take control of menopause and live life your way!

Helen Breward

Front cover illustration by Hollie Hopkins

Orders: Please contact www.helenbreward.com/My-Menopause

You can also order via the email address helen@helenbreward.com

ISBN: 978-1-9996622-0-2

First published 2018

Copyright © 2018 Helen Breward. All rights reserved.

All rights reserved. Apart from any permitted use under UK copyright law, no part of this publication may be reproduced or transmitted in any form or by any means, electronic or mechanical, including photocopying, recording, or any information, storage or retrieval system, without permission in writing from the publisher or under licence from the Copyright Licensing Agency Limited. Further details of such licenses (for reprographic reproduction) may be obtained from the Copyright Licensing Agency Ltd, Saffron House, 6-10 Kirby Street, London EC1N 8TS.

The information in this guide is not to be used as substitute for medical assistance, and the author cannot take responsibility for any health or dietary issues that arise from following her advice. If you require medical advice, then please seek out a qualified health or dietitian/nutritionalist. The author of this book is not medically or nutritionally trained, and all advice within this guide should be applied sensibly, and in accordance with your own health/diet situation.

Dedication

To Mum,

Even though you are no longer with us, you have still played a huge part in the creation of this book. You were truly a wise woman.

Colin my ever-loving husband, thank you for going along with all my crazy ideas, big and small, supporting and encouraging me through thick and thin. This has been an incredible journey, so far!

Acknowledgments

*To **Alison McQuillan**, thank you for being such fun and inspiration along the way. You were and still are a massive part of this whole journey. Mavis the proper cross fairy holds a very special place in my heart.*

*To **Claire Barrett**, who is a part of this book, who supports and encourages me, thank you for helping me to get this finished.*

*To **Craig Breward**, who's own determination to succeed reminds me never to give up, especially on those days when it would be so easy to do so. Thank you for teaching me so much and being you.*

*To **Dad**, thank you for all your unending support. It means so much to me, more than you know.*

*To **Jenny Holmes**, who not only has taught me meditation for many years but is also a great friend. Thank you so much Jenny for all your encouragement, laughter and teachings over the years.*

*To **Richard McMunn**, who said those three words I needed to hear 'I love it.' That was the moment that this book became reality for me. Thank you.*

*To **Sheila Granger**, who muttered those words, 'You know you have to write the book now don't you?' That comment set the words you are reading in to motion. Thank you so much for everything you do to help me; getting the Menopause Relief Programme off the ground for clients and therapists; becoming an international speaker and now author.*

CONTENTS

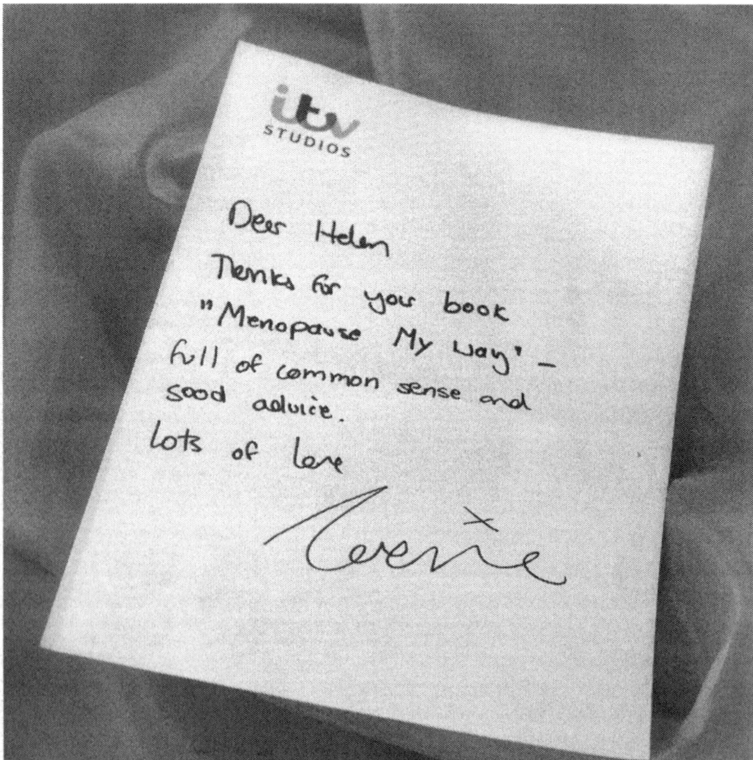

itv STUDIOS

Dear Helen

Thanks for your book "Menopause My Way" – full of common sense and good advice.

Lots of love

Live Life Your Way

Helen Breward

INTRODUCTION

There is a point in a woman's life when their body changes and menopause begins. For most women, this happens naturally. However, for a growing number, they are thrust prematurely into the depths of an early menopause. This can be for several reasons; hysterectomy, cancer treatment, chemically or as a preventative measure like the famous Hollywood actress Angelina Jolie. Either way, the result is the same, menopause. For example, imagine, you are going on holiday to Florida, you may take a plane flight, others may drive in a car, take a train or a bus. All the ladies in Florida arrived one way or another. How they all got there is immaterial, the outcome is the same; they are all in Florida.

Some women are lucky and have either none or very few symptoms, such as hot flushes, night sweats & sleeplessness. But there are a great many that are not quite so fortunate and really suffer. Arguably, hot flushes are probably the most common symptom when going through the menopause. But it seems to be the night sweats that cause the most disruption. Lack of good quality sleep can have a huge knock-on effect, as tiredness affects our ability to think, work, perform and do everyday tasks.

Choices for dealing with these symptoms seem to be limited to HRT or anti-depressants. More and more women are looking for an alternative, they don't want to or can't take HRT medication, but the issues are still there. I have taken a combined holistic and hypnosis approach to this issue. In my experience, taking supplements and specific foods make a subtle difference; tweaking your lifestyle adds further to that but it is when you add hypnosis to the mix that powerful results happen.

Hypnosis

Hypnosis is a deep focused relaxation, used by hypnotherapists like myself, to guide you into making changes that will benefit you. Your imagination is the most powerful gift you have, much stronger than willpower. I help individuals to visualise different things, to make those necessary changes. Just think about it for a moment, how often have we talked or thought ourselves into feeling ill because we didn't want to do something or go somewhere? Now imagine if you could do the opposite, focus on feeling great, really feel how you want to in the future - right now. Start believing and acting as if you were already there, feeling amazing.

The other side of my work is to teach individuals practical tools they can use if they need to, to help themselves with their feelings and certain situations. Backing up everything we do in a session with recordings to listen to every day, it only takes about 30 minutes, which help to embed all the changes we set in place; so that you move forward and progress between sessions. It's a working partnership. I can't make you do anything you don't want to. This is not stage-hypnosis, that is for entertainment. This is for your benefit and only your benefit.

HOW TO USE THIS BOOK

It is my intention that this book provides some ideas that you can try for yourself to help you take control or some control of the menopause and its symptoms. As always if you are concerned about your symptoms and health in any way, consult your Doctor.

Each Chapter starts off with a story or metaphor to do with that part of the menopause. This is because, in the world of hypnosis, metaphors and stories are a great way for clients to gain understanding, the subconscious part of the mind 'gets it' and who doesn't love a story? Besides, being an ex-primary school teacher, I love telling stories. So, yes, I'm also indulging myself here. Following on from the story is some relevant information that could help you practically.

Next, there is an activity for you to do, which is often something I ask clients to do, as I know they work very well for the vast majority of ladies.

Finally, are the key learning points from that Chapter.

There is also a free hypnosis recording for you to download from my website and a list of useful websites. www.helenbreward.com/menopause-my-way

If you would like to work with myself or one of my practitioners, please visit my website www.helenbreward.com/contact

Or to find one of my personally trained practitioners

www.helenbreward.com/find-a-practitioner

Why Hot Flushes?

I became a hypnotherapist during one of the most difficult and challenging times of my life. Whilst training, four members of my immediate family were diagnosed with cancer, my mother being terminal. The skills I developed helped not only myself, but those around me to cope. Looking back now, I know that I would not have got through that year in the way that I did without hypnosis.

But the menopause relief part of the story really began at my mother's funeral, when I clearly remember being in pain. This I put down to grief & stress at the time. However, several months later I was still in pain. To cut a long story short, after lots of trips to the Doctor, hospital and consultant, it was decided that I needed a hysterectomy. Did I mention that my house was in the middle of lots of building work, my daughter was due to have her first baby very soon and I was still a part-time primary school teacher? So, it's fair to say I had a lot going on.

As my operation date came closer, I began to think of the effects that this would have on my body; I have to say I was looking forward to no pain and no periods. I wasn't enamoured with the thought of hot flushes though. Somehow that thought stuck somewhere in my brain. If you can control pain with hypnosis, why not hot flushes? As you can imagine, I needed a lot of recovery time, not just physically but also mentally. As a family, we had all been through a huge amount in a short space of time. Losing my mum to cancer and welcoming a new granddaughter into the family would often send my emotions from deep grief and sadness to pure joy in the space of a heartbeat. As they say, grief takes the time it takes, there is no time-scale of when it should be over by. In fact, I think it's more a case of coming to terms with the loss and adjusting to the change within the family. My mum was truly the wise woman we all went to, who knew a vast amount and everyone.

So, it wasn't until a few years later that I actually put pen to paper, or in my case finger to keyboard. My curiosity had resurfaced stronger than ever, I just wanted to see if it was possible to turn down the heat of a hot flush. Over Christmas 2014 I finally switched on my laptop and spent 3 days writing all my ideas down. This very quickly became the menopause relief programme, MRP. The following week, I put 1 post on Facebook for volunteers to test out what I was convinced was possible. Through that 1 post, the notice was placed in the local newspaper and volunteers appeared.

Initial results from the trial were very encouraging. After the first session, 4 out of 5 of the ladies on the trial were able to turn down the heat of a hot flush to some extent. As the trial progressed, the results began to far exceed my original hopes. These ladies were not only able to turn the heat down, but also reduce the number of hot flushes occurring. I was amazed. The power of the mind never fails to surprise me.

One lady found that her hot flushes stopped at night. So, she was able to sleep through, getting a good night's rest. Other hot flushes had decreased in their intensity. All of this gave her a feeling of empowerment and control. Another lady saw a reduction from around 20 flushes a day to about 5 and she continues to improve. Overall, having positive strategies to use has given these ladies back their control. They feel like they are doing something about it. Instead of the menopause being in control, they are, which is very powerful.

Clinical trials conducted by Professor Gary Elkins of the Baylor Institute in America, published a paper in 2012 outlining his results concerning the effectiveness of hypnosis upon hot flushes. The findings were very similar to my own, or I should say mine mirrored those of the Baylor Institute. They reported that the ladies using hypnosis were able to reduce the heat and the number of occurrences of hot flushes, with continued improvements the longer hypnosis was used. This trial backs up everything I had thought, said and hoped, which means it's not just a hypnotherapist in Swindon spouting on about how fantastic hypnosis is. It provides credibility.

Since then I have:

- Had an article written about this work in the national glossy magazine Spirit & Destiny 2015.
- Many press releases in the local papers.
- Written & recorded a full training programme for other therapists to use.
- Been invited to present my work at the Canadian Hypnotherapy Conference 2016.
- Trained therapists in 8 different countries to use my work.
- Presented at the Hypnothoughts Live Conference in Las Vegas 2017
- Presented at the Hypnosense Conference in London 2017
- Helped many individual women to control their menopause.
- Worked internationally with clients and therapists.

- Written and published this book 'My Menopause, My Way'

That's a lot in 3 years. I could never have predicted that my curiosity would have taken off like this, taken me to so many places and met so many wonderful people. It is also fair to say that none of this would have happened without the support of colleagues who helped me to step out of my comfort zone and encouragement from family.

Looking ahead to the future, that's simple; always spreading the message that you can do something about it. You can take control.

Let the past be
a springboard for
the future...

a brighter future

Helen Breward

CHAPTER 1

In the Beginning

Chapter 1 - In the Beginning

Sitting in my garden, my quiet place, next to the waterfall beneath a big tall willow tree; the sun shines delicately through the leaves and branches giving a mix of dappled shade. Perfect. I find my silence, my peace. The world just stops for a time. It holds its breath while I just sit and be. While I recharge, enjoying the silence, just me.

Places like this send out a beacon of peace and tranquillity to all those sensitive and in need. I know before long I'll be joined, like bees drawn to honey, my daughter and granddaughters will find me here. A smile creeps across my face at the thought. So, I enjoy a few minutes of peace and silence, being at one with nature for a time…

With eyes closed, I hear excited voices shouting "Grandma" my heart jumps, swells with joy. Eyes open, I see two little blonde heads, big beaming smiles running towards me with arms open wide. The best love of all as they leap into my arms. Looking up, I see how my daughter has grown into such a beautiful woman. It seems only a moment ago when she was that little blonde head running at her grandma. She's loving and caring, stronger than she knows. Filled with, yet, undiscovered talents, abilities and capabilities all waiting to be uncovered. I smile. Setting down a little body on each knee, daughter by my side, I find peace, a different kind of peace.

"Tell us a story about the wise apple tree Grandma" glancing at my daughter, I take a deep breath and begin…

Long, long ago when the earth was full of magic and wonder, when all things were possible, Mother Nature sat beside a young sapling telling her about the wise apple tree. About how she grew up with such splendid views that take your breath away. As she looked out across the lush green countryside, how beautiful the bushes and other trees were. The wide variety of flowers in every colour you can imagine, so vivid and alive, tall trees ranging from majestic red woods to graceful weeping willows, so much beauty all around. And the animals, deer bring their young in the spring, rabbits so full of bounce, young foxes playing at sunset. Visits from birds of such beauty and exotic colours to those so plain they can hardly be seen. Young lovers hold hands, children play; others sit quietly, soaking up the peace beneath the branches. Magnificent sunsets to mark the end of a day, full of glowing yellows, oranges and blushing pinks that all say, 'what a great day'. Darkness prevails for a while, but it's never completely dark with the moon shining brightly accompanied by bright silvery stars that light the night sky. Finally, the dark inky blue and silver gives way to spectacular blues, golden yellows, cerise pinks that announce a new day full of promise, adventure and surprise. A new day dawns; a fresh start.

Mother Nature continued to talk about how the young apple tree blossomed brightly and spectacularly with delicate pink flowers, with a beautiful golden centre, each and every year. The big, round, black and yellow bumble bees that collected pollen from each flower, leaving behind a little from other trees, setting in motion new life, new apple trees. How interesting the bumble bees were to watch, because they really shouldn't be able to fly, just that no one has told them that, they don't know that they can't, so they do. They open their wings and just fly without even thinking about it, they expect to be able to do it, so they can. How the rosy red apples grew into such sweet and juicy fruit, in such abundance that it overwhelmed each branch, so much so that they would bow right down to touch the earth. This continued for many, many seasons. As the years rolled by the apple tree grew older and wiser, learned, watched and listened. It slowly began to produce fewer and fewer blossoms and fewer and fewer apples, until one year none grew at all. Now, all the other trees around were totally dismayed. But the wise apple tree was happy…

"Have I not blossomed each and every year for the last forty years? Have I not given a great abundance of juicy red apples to everyone around? Now is my time to rest and watch over you; to guide and help you; to offer shade and shelter to the young trees, to all living things, whatever they need and can find beneath my canopy as I stand tall, strong and welcoming. My life, my true purpose is only just beginning." She replied with a smile.

"But Grandma wasn't the wise apple tree sad to not grow apples anymore?" asked Melissa, the eldest.

"Why would she be sad? She is so much more than just growing apples. That is just one part of her, one part of her life that's changed. Everything changes. Change is good. It means growth, development and moving forward to new things."

I could see that Melissa was thinking about this, and smiled to myself, knowing that she would ponder over it again later, probably in the quiet of her bedroom. Other questions would likely arise in the days and weeks ahead.

The wise apple tree continued to talk about the love, joy and happiness she felt as children would swing so high on her branches, giggling and laughing. Having fun, gaining confidence, balance, learning to swing higher and higher; so much more than just a swing. How friends and lovers would sit and talk, hold hands, discover a new friendship, a new connection beneath its shelter. Some come and sit alone, but we are never alone, contemplating their life, their problems, themselves. Some sob. Some just sit and be at one with themselves and nature. As she protects, shelters, offers a safe place to be, a safe haven to talk, to let it all out with no judgment, no comment, no harsh words, no criticism, just love and compassion. They let go of their troubles. They find peace and solace. Nature shows us how to heal ourselves, all we need to do is look, watch, learn and copy. Follow the messages and clues Mother Nature has sprinkled all around us. Just like a treasure hunt.

My daughter looks at me with understanding and smiles, while the granddaughters giggle excitedly

"We love treasure hunts."

Always one step ahead, Melissa asks

"And does the wise apple tree show the people and other apple trees how to breathe, just like you do?"

"Of course, she does, just by doing it herself. Do you remember what I said about watching and learning?" The girls nod in reply.

"Mother Nature is very subtle with her clues and messages. They are clearly there for everyone to see, but only the observant and wise will truly see them and understand the treasure and use it to heal themselves."

I could see Melissa thinking and looking closely around her.

Then she proceeds to show me how to breathe, repeating back to me my own familiar words.

"A big deep breath in through your nose Grandma, hold it and count to four. Then let it out through your mouth, slowly, steadily until it's all gone. Do this anytime you feel uncomfortable or hot Grandma. I know you get a little hot sometimes."

It's at that point, I suddenly understand, completely understand that even when I'm gone I'll still be here, as all four of us repeat the breathing together. Handing down knowledge and wisdom to two more generations of women and however many they, in turn, pass it on to, not just their family but friends and acquaintances. Just like ripples on a pond spreading far and wide. We are truly eternal.

Rise with the sun,
hold your head high,
embrace the day

Helen Breward

Information

It's a known fact that when women reach a certain age their reproductive system slows down, the Perimenopause, and eventually stops working, the menopause. This is a natural part of life and happens to every woman. Perimenopause is the slowing down and leading into menopause, where periods have stopped for a year. After a year with no periods, you are then described medically as being post menopause i.e. you have completed the menopause. Generally speaking, most ladies consider this phase to be 'In or going through the menopause.' When their symptoms stop or disappear, then they consider themselves post-menopausal. To me, it seems that the medical definition implies that all symptoms have stopped by the end of 12 months. In my experience, personally and as a hypnotherapist helping a lot of women with their hot flushes, these symptoms can continue for years. In some extreme cases I have heard about, into the late 70's. However, there is also the other end of the spectrum where there are no symptoms.

The average age for menopause is 51, as always there are many exceptions to this.

There isn't a magic button that flips on your 51st birthday. This is the phase when your body is adjusting to the hormone imbalance created by lower oestrogen and progesterone levels, a period of readjustment.

These are some of the common signs that this process has begun:

- Irregular periods (Perimenopause)

- Periods have stopped
- Irritability
- Mood swings
- Anxiety
- Depression
- Panic attacks
- Feel hotter, like the heating has been turned up a bit.
- Hot flushes
- Dry skin
- Aching joints
- Low or no libido/sex drive
- Hair thinning
- More facial hair
- Tender breasts
- Weight gain

If your sign/symptom is not listed, then don't worry, the list is huge. You know your body better than anyone else. If you are concerned at all, please seek medical advice from your Doctor.

Action

Practise the breathing technique daily.

Use this breathing method as soon as you notice a hot flush coming on or when you get that tingle or sign it's about to happen.

1. Breathe in cool air through your nose. Really imagine being cool, or a time when you were.

2. Hold your breath and count to four.
3. Slowly and controlled, breathe out the excessive heat through your mouth.
4. Repeat if necessary.

Feel yourself calming down and cooling down.

This breathing is useful for many things not just to relieve hot flushes. So, if you feel anxious, stressed, have cravings or any emotion you don't like or want, do the breathing as soon as you notice it. It is much easier to nip it in the bud at the beginning, rather than when it has escalated to great heights.

Key Learning Points

- Find your peaceful place and use it regularly.
- It is said that if your last thoughts are positive as you fall asleep, you will wake up feeling positive.
- At the end of every day, as you drift off to sleep be grateful for three things, no matter how small.
- Recognise that change happens all the time. Change is good.
- Know that your role in life is changing as the needs of those near and dear grow and look to you for support in a different way.
- You are the wise woman.
- There are many signs and symptoms of the menopause such as - no periods, irritability, mood swings, anxiety, depression, panic attacks, hot flushes, low libido/sex drive to name a few.
- Not every woman has these symptoms and, in all likelihood, won't have all of them, maybe just one or two. Some won't have any at all.
- Practise the breathing technique every day. Breathe in cool air through your nose. Really imagine being cool or a time when you were.

  Hold your breath and count to four.

  Slowly and controlled breathe out the excessive heat through your mouth.

  Repeat if necessary.

- Your attitude towards the menopause and the changes taking place will make a world of difference to you.
- Above all THINK POSITIVELY. BE POSITIVE

CHAPTER 2

When the Heat Rises

The lady in the mirror is a wise woman,

she is an amazing person.

Helen Breward

Chapter 2 - When the Heat Rises

When the earth was first created and full of magic, Mother Nature didn't always get it right. Adjustments were needed here and there. Some things were in the wrong place, or too tight or simply not enough space for such a grand plan. This was how it was with the hills and mountains, packed tightly. Now Mother Nature was very busy and put this on a 'To do' list. We all know how long they can be. Some things just don't get done. So, like children squashed in the back of a car, the hills and mountains would move a bit, pushing one another out or up, jostling for the best position, all wanting to face the sun as much as possible, to feel that delicious warmth on the earth and rocks. As the pressure built up, the heat from the very core of the earth began to rise. Only a little bit at first, hardly noticeable, but rise it did, whilst the 'To do' list continued to grow.

One day, Mother Nature had just finished adding several more things to the list, when she noticed, actually noticed just how long it was. Looking out across the vast landscape of hills and mountains in the distance, she closed her eyes, put her bare feet on the ground and tuned in. Focusing on the animals, birds, the trees, plants and finally the hills and mountains. Nature is the very soul of the earth. At first, she felt the deep harmony all around, but slowly as she focused on the hills and mountains a sense of unrest, a bit like a tiny speck of dirt on a white cloth, became noticeable. Of course, once you notice it, that's all you can see. So, tuning in even more on that spot, she began to feel just how much unrest there really was, all jostling for position, pushing and shoving, tempers rising. This was the moment of realisation that something had to be done.

Help was needed. So, being immensely creative, Mother Nature took some of the magic from the earth and created fairies and elves. They were responsible for keeping order and the day to day running of things. Making sure the grand plan was in order and running smoothly. Caretakers if you like. Some, mainly elves, were assigned the hills to the south, others the mountains to the north, east or west, whilst some took care of the rivers and seas. But the most magical of all the fairies were to watch over the animals, the birds, those that lived in the sea or on the land. To start off with this worked well, peace and order reigned.

However, after a while, a few grumblings began from one or two of the elves.

“It’s not fair, why should those stuck-up fairies get the best jobs? The most interesting ones?”

The elves were ignored for a time, after all, who doesn’t have a little moan now and then? But... this moaning continued and slowly began to spread to other elves in other corners of the earth. Unhappiness was spreading, like a virus. Because they were too busy moaning about work and how unfair things were, their own responsibilities were being neglected more and more. This carried on for several years. For the mountains being squashed and squeezed the pressure was building more and more, rising higher and higher, forced into smaller and smaller spaces. All was not well.

The moaning elves formed groups, which became bigger and bigger. They would march to places where the fairies lived and worked, getting louder and louder, until it could not be ignored any longer. Talks were held but arguments would quickly break out, each side shouting louder and louder trying to be heard by the other. Frustration and anger ruled as neither side would compromise at all. No one was listening, just shouting louder and louder about their own point of view, their own perspective. No one stopped to consider how the other side felt. They were too focused on being right. Neither side would compromise at all. It's probably true to say that all the elves really wanted were better working conditions and recognition. They wanted to feel important, worthwhile like they were making a difference to the earth, just like they saw the fairies doing. And the fairies didn't want to give up their status. A stalemate ensued.

Meanwhile, responsibilities on all sides were completely neglected. Pressure grew, and the animals were getting wilder and wilder, doing their own thing, unchecked.

Until one day, when everything became too much. I mean everything, the arguments, bad tempers, the pressure in the mountains, the wildness of the animals, it was all too much. Total chaos ruled.

For one of the mountains in the west, this was the final straw. Letting out the most tremendous loud roar, it blew its top. Literally blew its top right off. All the years of built up pressure and heat from the earth's core finally popped like a champagne cork on New Year's Eve, spewing up and out high into the sky, raining down on the earth below. Hot molten lava flowed out of the hole and down the sides of the mountain in all directions, burning the plants and trees, animals and birds and scalding the earth. Everything that could move took cover as best as possible. Arguments were forgotten in an instant and help freely given. Nothing escaped the wrath of the mountain as it roared for days. The devastated earth glowed red hot. After what seemed like an age, the intense heat began to fade, the flowing lava began to slow down, and the loud roar gradually became a soft moan.

Eventually, calmness and peace slowly began to return. Coolness began to creep over the land again. A gentle breeze blew, dissipating the remaining heat as a sense of normality returned. The first volcano had been created.

One of the good things that happened was it stopped the fairies and elves in their tracks. It made them all realise just how important each one of them was as they surveyed the aftermath. Total devastation, the earth was barren, burned, black and grey. Some trees remained, blackened and burned, no longer the tall, lush green beauties they once were; a shadow of their former selves. A stunned silence full of shame, regret and grief followed. Over the next few weeks, the consequences of their actions became abundantly clear. A truce was formed. Lessons were being learned not just by the Elves & Fairies but all the creatures, the very earth itself. Things had to change. A compromise had to be made for the good of all living things. Or the earth would eventually destroy itself in a bubbling river of intense, red-hot molten lava, wiping out everything in its path.

It was time to consult Mother Nature. After much discussion and negotiation that lasted several long days and nights, a compromise was finally agreed. From this moment on, the Elves became men, taking on a role of greater physical strength and supporting the Fairies. In turn, the Fairies took on the burden of heat and became women, to relieve the pressure from the volcanoes. This was a huge weight to bear, so Mother Nature postponed the heat until each woman had finished having children, until they were older and wiser. It was hoped that when the heat came women would have knowledge and experience on their side to help them. Maybe even know how to control it and stop it, cool it down, until all the heat has gone, dissipated for good. Mother Nature explained to both sides that great patience would be required. There would be times when irritability ruled, when moodiness reigned, when tears flowed unchecked and heat burst forth like a volcano erupting. Women would need support to get through this phase. It wasn't to last forever, just a short time.

Realising the enormity of their tasks, their new purposes both sides shook hands, sat down and chatted. A new bond was forming. A new kind of peace began to settle over the earth. The long road to recovery had begun. New shoots were sprouting as a faint, fresh green hue spread across the land.

From that moment on men and women found a new way to be, they supported each other, their bond became closer and tighter. Alongside this another even stronger connection was forged, that was between women, who also vowed to support each other through thick and thin, no matter what. After all, who understands better than a woman who has already travelled that path? So, if from time to time couples argued or fell out, women would always have support from each other.

Breathe deeply
head high
Be your own hero

Helen Breward

Information - Your Hormones

Oestrogen and progesterone are the two main hormones we focus on with menopause, although we should not forget the third one testosterone. To understand the popular theory of oestrogen dominance, it is necessary to understand the roles of oestrogen and progesterone. If you look at the chart below, you will begin to see how these two hormones work together and balance each other out.

Oestrogen	**Progesterone**
Builds the lining of the womb	Maintains the lining of the womb
Headaches, anxiety, depression	Acts as a natural anti-depressant, calms anxiety
Weight gain and increased body fat	Helps the body to use the fat as energy.
Poor sleep patterns	Promotes sleep
Low or no libido/sex drive	Increases libido/sex drive
Higher risk of breast cancer	Helps with the prevention of breast cancer.
Hinders blood sugar control	Regulates blood sugar control

These are just a few of the many roles of these hormones. You may recognise some of them in yourself. In menopause, progesterone levels drop quite quickly, whilst oestrogen falls at a slower pace. Thus, oestrogen can become unbalanced by much lower progesterone levels. So, looking at the chart if, for example, you start to experience anxiety, depression, low sex drive and weight gain it could indicate that your progesterone levels are too low, leaving a degree of oestrogen dominance.

These vitamins and minerals are generally good for menopause:

Vitamin C – good for hot flushes, the immune system, incontinence.

Vitamin B's – production of red blood cells, production of new body cells, convert food into energy, increase energy, improve mood, help with anxiety, skin, hair, production of hormones.

Omega 3 – good for the brain, heart and eyes. These are also good for promoting the production of progesterone:

Zinc - is also required in the production of progesterone and testosterone.

Magnesium - helps to keep the hormones balanced, so eating foods rich in magnesium will help with progesterone production & levels.

B6 - is required to produce progesterone

Hormone balance is a delicate thing and varies from person to person, this is just a guide. As always if you are concerned, consult your Doctor.

There is a small part of the brain called the hypothalamus which controls and regulates many of the body's functions; hormones being one of them, temperature control another. So, when a decrease in oestrogen occurs, this is detected by the brain as too much heat and therefore, employs the cooling system, those rivers of sweat.

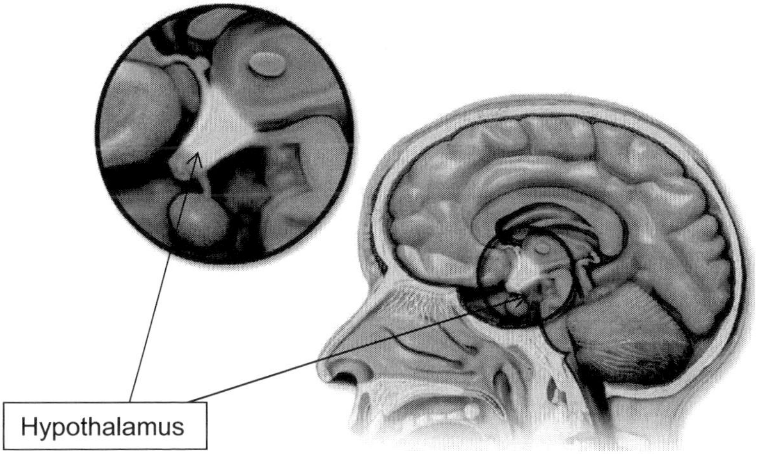

Blausen.com staff. "Blausen gallery 2014". *Wikiversity Journal of Medicine.* DOI:10.15347/wjm/2014.010. ISSN 20018762

Activity

Start to notice when you have hot flushes, what you are doing at the time, what you have just eaten or drank. You are starting to look for common triggers that set off some of your hot flushes e.g., a hot meal and a hot drink (two hot things together), wine, red in particular, stress, rushing around and certain foods. When you suspect that something could be a trigger, change it or stop doing it for at least a few days, by then you will likely know if it is one of your causes.

Find ways that you enjoy to relieve the pressure. Be more active, take an exercise class, go for a walk amongst the trees, meditate or do something just for yourself. Make a habit of taking time for yourself every day, even if it is only 10 minutes, it will serve you well.

Key Learning Points

- Use all your knowledge and wisdom to help yourself through this transition in life.
- Learn from other wise women that have already trodden this path.
- Don't be too hard on yourself. If you wouldn't say it to a child, then don't say It to yourself.
- Seek out support from other women, family and friends.
- Remember oestrogen and progesterone tend to balance each other out.
- Progesterone levels drop much quicker than oestrogen, so you may have an imbalance.
- Eat nutritious foods to help your body produce the hormones that it needs. You will feel better.
- Some of the things that progesterone does is to act as a natural anti-depressant, help your body to use up the fat and increases sex drive.
- One of the things the hypothalamus does is to control body temperature. It is affected by hormone imbalance,

detects it as too much heat and sends out rivers of sweat to cool the body down.

- Start to notice your triggers. Be aware.
- Be more active, take an exercise class, go for a walk.
- Taking time out for yourself every day would be great, even if it is only 10 minutes.

CHAPTER 3

Long Hot Nights

This is your time

Embrace it

Enjoy the journey

Helen Breward

Chapter 3 - Long Hot Nights

Thinking about those uncomfortable night sweats reminded me about a particularly hot summer, many years ago when Alice was a young girl. You remember those lovely hot summer days, with temperatures soaring into the 30's (Fahrenheit 85+) and even higher. Wearing light cotton clothes, shirts, dresses, shorts or maybe skirts. Where the children played all day long in shorts & tee shirts, spending the afternoons in paddling pools, playing in the freezing cold water. Giggling and squealing with delight. Such fun.

Now, we all know in the summer, hot days tend to be followed by hot nights and in Britain, we don't have the luxury of air conditioning. So, hot, sticky and stuffy nights can be uncomfortable, making it hard to get a good night's sleep.

One such hot, sticky and stuffy night Alice was finding it very difficult to get to sleep. She had had a fantastic day playing with her friend Shelly. Pretending to swim in the paddling pool, splashing water over each other, running in and out of a garden sprinkler, oh what fun it had been … and best of all a huge water fight, with the two families, finished off the day. She was exhausted. Oh, but what fun. A great day to remember. But she really needed to sleep now. It was so hot and sticky.

As Alice lay there, she began to remember & relive the day again. That first dip in the pool with her big toe, squealing because it was *sooooo* cold. As she remembered this a big shiver ran through her body. She began to cool down. Then, she thought about how she and Shelly had stood huddled together in the middle of the pool, shivering. How their feet & toes had gone numb with the ice-cold water, how delightful it was. Cooling down in such a fun way. Alice remembered the feeling of the cooling shower from the garden sprinkler landing on her head, trickling down her back, cascading over her front. So wonderful, so cooling, so refreshing. As she remembered the day, she noticed she actually felt cooler. So, what other cooling memories could she think about?

Ah, that lovely, long, cold drink of iced water that mum had given them, to cool them both down. Why hadn't she thought of that before? How the ice cubes had tinkled and clinked in that delightful way on the side of the glass as she picked it up. The coolness of the glass on the lips... oh then, that ice cold liquid swirling around your mouth, just before it travels to the back of your throat. And just for a few seconds that cold, numb feeling as it spreads down into your tummy, into your body. Icy fingers like tentacles reaching out far and wide, cooling as they go... Just thinking about it now, instantly made Alice feel much cooler, much calmer and much more relaxed. And that second mouthful... clink, as the ice touched the glass... even colder this time, as the cool refreshing water again swirled around her mouth. Spreading its icy tentacles even further this time, cooling her even more, relaxing her even more, calming her even more. Finally, drifting off to sleep, feeling cool, calm and relaxed.

Now, Alice had learned something very valuable that night. She had realised that she was in control, that she could change how she felt and how her body reacted, just by thinking about it. WOW! So, the next night, she did the same thing again, focusing on that long cold ice water, as it touched the lips and swirled around the mouth, touching her tummy and spreading like Jack Frost through her body. Instantly cooling her down, I mean physically cooling her down.

Over the next few weeks, she continued to do this, remembering and seeing herself drinking that iced water, in her mind. Drinking it in the daytime and remembering, reliving it at night. Alice couldn't believe it, it actually worked, it was so simple, so easy. But more importantly, she noticed that the more she did this, the easier and stronger, more powerful it became. WOW! She was in control of her mind and body.

From that night onwards, from that moment onwards Alice always slept peacefully, always slept coolly and restfully throughout each night, waking in the morning feeling fully refreshed, revitalised and full of energy.

Focus Your

Incredible

Imagination

on being

Cool

Calm

and

Comfortable

Helen Breward

Information

In my experience, it is the night sweats that tend to cause the most disruption, as sleep is interrupted. Some of the cases I have worked with have experienced this up to 6 or 7 times a night, with the extreme being a shower, change of nightwear and bedclothes.

Now, if this happens once in the week we can tend to recover quickly with very little effect on us or our lives. However, when it happens every night, for weeks and months and years you can begin to understand the huge impact that would have on your life and you physically.

There is often a difference between the hot flushes you have in the day to those in the night. Quite often the night ones will start in a different place, more intense and can last longer. A further two types of hot flushes seem to be very common and these are the ones that I call, changing state flushes. By that I mean when you are physically transitioning from being active to relaxing and drifting into sleep. Then again in the morning when you wake up and become active again.

One of the ways you can help this is by taking a few minutes to relax and prepare your mind and body for sleep; unwind, read, just lie in bed and think about the best bits from the day. Positive thinking has a tremendous impact on your menopause. In the morning it's about allowing yourself a few minutes to 'come around', wake up before you leap out of bed. Okay, gracefully swing your legs to the floor, stretch and stand up.

Action

As mentioned in the previous Chapter there are certain foods we can eat that have the vitamins and minerals which are generally thought to be good for menopause support. See Chapter 4 for the food guide.

Start to be aware of your lifestyle, stresses, the food you are eating and what you are drinking. There are likely to be things that are triggering hot flushes and night sweats. Alcohol in the evening can often be a trigger for a night sweat or a sweaty night. Part of the process of managing your menopause your way is to be aware of your own personal triggers, things that you can do something about. The other part is using your powerful imagination to help control your body, which is the purpose of these stories, to give you some ideas on how to do that.

Key Learning Points

- Start to notice what you are eating and drinking in the evening. Try eliminating one thing for a couple of nights and see if that makes a difference.
- Alcohol is a common trigger for many women. If you do like a tipple, it may be that a different drink does not set you off.
- Eat good, nutritious food that supports your body.
- How busy are you? How stressful is your life right now? Stress in particular, is a massive trigger for hot flushes. Make tweaks to your lifestyle. Use some of the activities and points in this book, you can help yourself to manage stress better.
- Take time at the end of the day to mentally and physically wind down and prepare for sleep.
- Take a few minutes to wake up, stretch and get out of bed in the morning.
- Use your powerful imagination to help your body feel cool, calm and comfortable. Your mind is so powerful and can do so much, put it to good use.

CHAPTER 4

Two Trees

Your mind is

more powerful

than you know

Use it wisely

Helen Breward

Chapter 4 - Two Trees

Two trees stood tall in the middle of a valley, side by side. They were offspring from the same tree, sisters, if you like. As young saplings they were flexible, bending with the wind, stretching up to the very sun itself, growing this way and that, learning the ways of nature. Their bark was smooth and perfect, blemish free. It had such a beautiful golden-brown glow to it, that many passers-by would comment

“What beautiful trees. Look at the amazing colour of the trunk.”

For many years the sisters enjoyed their youth, their natural beauty, flexibilities and abilities to adapt to Mother Nature and the changing valley around them. They always enjoyed the shelter of the lush green valley, marvelling at the hills surrounding them. The way they gently rolled up and swept down into the valley, like a big blanket protecting them, keeping them warm in the winter from the cold and snow. In the summer the many shades of green were breathtaking, so many different hues, too many to count.

As the years rolled on, the sisters grew tall and were proud to be the big magnificent trees that they were. Their colours changed, their trunks changed, their shape changed, their very branches changed. But it didn’t happen overnight, it was a slow gradual process over time. One that was hardly noticeable. Many things changed that were unseen, like the gathering of nutrients from the earth. But even more subtly, were the actual nutrients that the sisters required. You see, when they were young saplings they needed a certain blend of nourishment that would aid growth and suppleness. As they matured into beautiful young trees, they needed a different blend to not only maintain their magnificence and beauty but to reproduce new seeds packed full of potential to become equally as big and radiant. This changed again as the sisters became older, slowly reproducing fewer seeds until they finally stopped altogether. When this happened their blend of nutrients changed, they required more of some, less of others and some new. Their branches were more brittle, some easily snapping off. They became less flexible in the wind and feeling more irritable, not always enjoying the wondrous landscape in which they lived.

One particularly windy day, Beryl the older sister, by a few hours, was having a bad day. She moaned and creaked in the wind. She felt grumpy and irritable. Everything was wrong in her world. After spending, what seemed like all day to Cybil her sister, moaning, complaining and generally snipping about all her ailments Beryl finally stopped, ran out of steam. As she began to cry, she looked across at Cybil and noticed that she was gently bending with the wind. She could faintly hear little creaks now and again. When she listened to herself, there was a different sound. Frequent loud creaks and cracks, as the wind battered around her. Why?

For several days Beryl watched Cybil. She studied her sister closely, noticing little things, little differences. Wondering why? They came from the same tree, germinated at the same time, within a few hours of each other. So, why? The more she watched, studied and observed her sister the more curious she became. Until one day Beryl just had to say something. It wasn't fair that Cybil seemed to be so much younger and better than her. What was her secret?

"Why don't you creak and crack as loudly and as much as I do?"

Cybil smiled to herself, she had noticed all the watching Beryl had been doing, so was waiting for her to speak up.

"I have two secrets," said Cybil

"Do you remember when we were young and learned to dance in the wind? The fun we used to have, even with the gentlest of breezes, dancing with just the very top branches. How we'd let the leaves dance to their own tune. I could feel, really feel the music, the song of the wind deep down in my trunk. And the most amazing thing is that the song is different every time, what a fantastic gift the wind gives us every day. I am grateful for this because it not only keeps my trunk, branches and leaves supple and flexible but just as importantly, on those days when my spirit wanes and is low, I listen, really listen for the song. When it comes, I breathe in deeply; as I let it out I relax and allow myself to get lost in the rhythm of the song, lost in the music. Quite simply I have never stopped dancing in the wind."

Beryl was quiet for a time, trying to remember just when it was she had stopped dancing in the wind. A question began to form in her mind, the answer worried her, or what she thought was the answer. In the end, she just had to ask.

"Once you have stopped dancing, is it possible to start again?"

With tenderness in her eyes, Cybil replied with one word

"Yes"

"How? I don't hear the song like you, I can't move like you."

"It's actually quite easy, but it does require patience, dedication and time."

Eager to know more Beryl waited for her sister to show her what to do. For the first time in... well she couldn't remember, Beryl began to feel lightness in her spirit, a small voice of hope. She liked that feeling, allowing herself to just enjoy it for a while longer.

During the next few weeks, Cybil began to teach Beryl how to listen carefully to the wind's song. How to relax and move gently to the rhythm of the music. At first, there was no change, Beryl was as stiff as ever. But slowly, very slowly she noticed she was moving easier, more and her trunk was changing. She could hear the song on the wind. She could feel the rhythm deep down in her spirit. But most of all she felt so much better than she had in years. She, Beryl was dancing in the wind and it felt good.

"What's your second secret? You said you had two secrets. The first is dancing in the wind. So, what is the second?"

"Nourishment, I take in different nutrients now, to the ones from years ago when we were producing seeds. I listen carefully to my trunk, my branches and leaves, but just as importantly I look at them. I notice the colours, blemishes, how supple the leaves, twigs and branches are. Simply, I take notice of how I look, not in a 'am I beautiful?' way but a 'how healthy am I?' way."

Cybil wasn't sure that it made sense, but seeing Beryl nodding, she then carried on.

"Then I send out a message to the roots telling them what I need from the earth. So, they search, collect and absorb just the right nutrients in the right amounts for me. But also, I have that same conversation with the leaves. So, they know just what and how much to soak up from the rays of the sun."

Thinking for a moment, Beryl asked

"But how do you know what you need and how much?"

"Do you remember when we talked about listening for the wind's song? This is the same, only you are listening to yourself; your trunk, branches, leaves, roots, your spirit. They all have a rhythm. When everything is working together as one, there is harmony. So, you need to listen and look at yourself, remember what your harmony feels, sounds and looks like; your song. If there is discord, you need to feel for it, ask "what do you need?" The answer will come; the roots and leaves will then seek and gather."

Over the next few months, Beryl worked hard to understand her song, her harmony. Again, a question began to develop in her mind until she could hold on to it no longer.

"How do you know all this stuff about nutrients, harmony and your song, it's so hard?"

"Each seed is packed full of knowledge of things already learned and curiosity to seek out new things to discover new ways."

"Yes, I remember putting those into my seeds," said Beryl.

"And?"

Beryl's mind was blank. Patiently Cybil waited for understanding to dawn...

"Those seeds will grow up with that knowledge and curiosity inside them?"

Beryl was unsure of herself, not really knowing what Cybil was getting at.

"That's right they will, and it never leaves them."

Cybil again waited...

Suddenly, after what seemed like a whole season, Beryl shouted

"Oh, oh, I've got it. It's already inside of me, I have the answers. I'm just like you, but I'd forgotten that's all."

A huge smile spread out across her trunk.

After that moment she could hear her song, her rhythm. She could talk to any and all parts herself. She even began to listen to Mother Nature, just like Cybil.

Life was so much better now for Beryl. She was flexible and harmony prevailed. Those dark and miserable times were, gone. That's not to say she never feels low sometimes, she does. But on those days, she listens even more carefully for the wind's song and dances her heart out. Her most favourite type of day is a strong blustery wind with the sun shining brightly. Oh, how she dances on those days. You would think she was a young sapling again and in her spirit, she is.

Have fun

Be active

and

Dance every day

Helen Breward

Information

Weight gain in menopause is quite common. In Chapter 2, the effects of oestrogen and progesterone are shown in a chart. One of the effects of oestrogen is that it increases body fat, normally progesterone balances it out and helps the body to use that fat as energy. However, during menopause progesterone levels drop quite quickly, which in this case can affect the body's ability to convert fat to energy. Nutrients like vitamin C, Zinc, Magnesium, B6 and vitamin E are thought to promote the production of progesterone, which in turn will raise your levels and so aid the body to use fat as energy. It's about providing the right building blocks to produce hormones. After all, if you were building a house and used poor quality sand and cement the bricks would be less able to stay in place and hold each other up. Constant repairs would have to be made as the house increases in age and cement crumbles away. If good quality materials were used in the right quantities, the bricks would easily be able to hold up the house and do their job well; looking splendid and well cared for no matter the age. Of course, the odd bit of maintenance work may need to be done from time to time but with quality materials, all will be good for many years.

Good Nutrients – See Food Chart, which is by no means complete and full. Just some foods that are known to be high in specific nutrients.

Vitamin C

Zinc

Magnesium

B6

Vitamin E

Food Guide - Vitamins & Minerals

	Vitamin A Bones Best sources are from Beta-Carotene	**Vitamin B's** Production of red blood cells & new body cells, food into energy, mood, anxiety, skin, hair, hormones.	**Vitamin B6** production of progesterone, red blood cells & serotonin; low energy, depression & mood swings	**Vitamin B12** Making red blood cells & DNA, healthy nervous system, brain function & bones	**Vitamin C** Immune System, Hot Flushes, Incontinence	**Vitamin D** Bones Testosterone production.	**Vitamin E** Hot flushes Helps ease stress & depression	**Omega 3** Brain, heart, eyes, production of progesterone	**Zinc** Production of progesterone & testosterone; body's processes	**Magnesium** Hormone balance, production of progesterone & levels	**Calcium** Bones
Beef		●	●	●					●		
Beef liver / liver	●	●	●			●					
Chicken		●	●						●		
Ham		●									
Pork		●	●								
Poultry			●	●							
Lamb									●		
Turkey		●	●								
Meat				●							
Fish		●	● **Sword Fish**	●							
Fatty/oily fish						●		●			

Food Guide - Vitamins & Minerals

	Vitamin A Bones Best sources are from Beta-Carotene	**Vitamin B's** Production of red blood cells & new body cells, food into energy, mood, anxiety, skin, hair, hormones.	**Vitamin B6** production of progesterone	**Vitamin B12** Making red blood cells & DNA, healthy nervous system, brain function.	**Vitamin C** Immune System, Hot Flushes, Incontinence	**Vitamin D** Bones Testosterone production.	**Vitamin E** Hot flushes Helps ease stress & depression	**Omega 3** Brain, heart, eyes, production of progesterone	**Zinc** Production of progesterone & testosterone	**Magnesium** Hormone balance, production of progesterone & levels	**Calcium** Bones
Fish liver oils / cod liver oil		●				●		●			
Shell fish				●			●		●		
Clams				●							
Crab				●					●		
Mussels				●							
Oysters								●	●		
Seafood			●								
Anchovy								●			
Halibut			●							●	
Herring			●					●			
Mackerel								●		●	

Food Guide - Vitamins & Minerals

	Vitamin A Bones Best sources are from Beta-Carotene	**Vitamin B's** Production of red blood cells & new body cells, food into energy, mood, anxiety, skin, hair, hormones.	**Vitamin B6** production of progesterone, red blood cells & serotonin; low energy, depression & mood swings	**Vitamin B12** Making red blood cells & DNA, healthy nervous system, brain function & bones	**Vitamin C** Immune System, Hot Flushes, Incontinence	**Vitamin D** Bones Testosterone production.	**Vitamin E** Hot flushes Helps ease stress & depression	**Omega 3** Brain, heart, eyes, production of progesterone	**Zinc** Production of progesterone & testosterone; body's processes	**Magnesium** Hormone balance, production of progesterone & levels	**Calcium** Bones
Salmon		●	●					●		●	
Sardines								●			●
Tuna / Cooked Tuna		●	●								
Canola Oil								●			
Caviar								●			
Butter	●					●	●				●
Cheese		●		●		●				● **Goats Cheese**	●
Eggs	●	●		●							
Egg Yolks						●					
Milk		●		●							●
Soya Milk		●	●								

Food Guide - Vitamins & Minerals

	Vitamin A Bones Best sources are from Beta-Carotene	**Vitamin B's** Production of red blood cells & new body cells, food into energy, mood, anxiety, skin, hair, hormones.	**Vitamin B6** production of progesterone, red blood cells & serotonin; low energy, depression & mood swings	**Vitamin B12** Making red blood cells & DNA, healthy nervous system, brain function & bones	**Vitamin C** Immune System, Hot Flushes, Incontinence	**Vitamin D** Bones Testosterone production.	**Vitamin E** Hot flushes Helps ease stress & depression	**Omega 3** Brain, heart, eyes, production of progesterone	**Zinc** Production of progesterone & testosterone; body's processes	**Magnesium** Hormone balance, production of progesterone & levels	**Calcium** Bones
Yogurt		●		●						●	●
Asparagus		●							●		
Avocado		●	●				●			●	
Bok Choy											●
Brussel Sprouts					●						
Broccoli	●	●			●		●		●		●
Cabbage					●						
Cauliflower					●						
Carrots	●									●	
Dark Green leafy Veg	●	●			●					●	

Food Guide - Vitamins & Minerals

	Vitamin A Bones Best sources are from Beta-Carotene	**Vitamin B's** Production of red blood cells & new body cells, food into energy, mood, anxiety, skin, hair, hormones.	**Vitamin B6** production of progesterone, red blood cells & serotonin; low energy, depression & mood swings	**Vitamin B12** Making red blood cells & DNA, healthy nervous system, brain function & bones	**Vitamin C** Immune System, Hot Flushes, Incontinence	**Vitamin D** Bones Testosterone production.	**Vitamin E** Hot flushes Helps ease stress & depression	**Omega 3** Brain, heart, eyes, production of progesterone	**Zinc** Production of progesterone & testosterone; body's processes	**Magnesium** Hormone balance, production of progesterone & levels	**Calcium** Bones
Green & Red Peppers	●		●		●						
Kale	●				●					●	●
Miso		●									
Mushroom		●				●			●		
Okra	●				●				●	●	●
Peas		●			●					●	
Potato		●	●		●						
Spinach	●	●	●		●		●		●	●	
Squash							●				
Squash (Winter)	●				●						

Food Guide - Vitamins & Minerals

	Vitamin A Bones Best sources are from Beta-Carotene	**Vitamin B's** Production of red blood cells & new body cells, food into energy, mood, anxiety, skin, hair, hormones.	**Vitamin B6** production of progesterone, red blood cells & serotonin; low energy, depression & mood swings	**Vitamin B12** Making red blood cells & DNA, healthy nervous system, brain function & bones	**Vitamin C** Immune System, Hot Flushes, Incontinence	**Vitamin D** Bones Testosterone production.	**Vitamin E** Hot flushes Helps ease stress & depression	**Omega 3** Brain, heart, eyes, production of progesterone	**Zinc** Production of progesterone & testosterone; body's processes	**Magnesium** Hormone balance, production of progesterone & levels	**Calcium** Bones
Sweet Potato	●				●		●				
Watercress											●
Apricots	●	●									
Bananas		●	●		●					●	
Tomato		●			●						
Berries		●			●						
Orange & Yellow Fruits	●	●			●						
Beans			●						●	●	
Chick Peas			●						●	●	●
Lentils		●								●	

Food Guide - Vitamins & Minerals

	Vitamin A Bones Best sources are from Beta-Carotene	**Vitamin B's** Production of red blood cells & new body cells, food into energy, mood, anxiety, skin, hair, hormones.	**Vitamin B6** production of progesterone, red blood cells & serotonin; low energy, depression & mood swings	**Vitamin B12** Making red blood cells & DNA, healthy nervous system, brain function & bones	**Vitamin C** Immune System, Hot Flushes, Incontinence	**Vitamin D** Bones Testosterone production.	**Vitamin E** Hot flushes Helps ease stress & depression	**Omega 3** Brain, heart, eyes, production of progesterone	**Zinc** Production of progesterone & testosterone; body's processes	**Magnesium** Hormone balance, production of progesterone & levels	**Calcium** Bones
Soya Beans			●					●		●	
Almond		●					●			●	●
Brazil Nuts										●	
Cashew									●	●	
Hazel Nuts							●				
Peanuts		●									
Pecan		●									
Walnuts			●					●			
Nuts		●							●		
Chia Seeds								●		●	
Flax Seeds/ Linseeds								●		●	

Food Guide - Vitamins & Minerals

	Vitamin A Bones Best sources are from Beta-Carotene	**Vitamin B's** Production of red blood cells & new body cells, food into energy, mood, anxiety, skin, hair, hormones.	**Vitamin B6** production of progesterone, red blood cells & serotonin; low energy, depression & mood swings	**Vitamin B12** Making red blood cells & DNA, healthy nervous system, brain function & bones	**Vitamin C** Immune System, Hot Flushes, Incontinence	**Vitamin D** Bones Testosterone production.	**Vitamin E** Hot flushes Helps ease stress & depression	**Omega 3** Brain, heart, eyes, production of progesterone	**Zinc** Production of progesterone & testosterone; body's processes	**Magnesium** Hormone balance, production of progesterone & levels	**Calcium** Bones
Pumpkin Seeds								●	●	●	●
Squash Seeds									●	●	
Sunflower Seeds			●				●			●	
Fortified Foods						●					
Fortified Whole Grain Cereals		●	●							●	
Wheat Germ							●		●		
Whole Grain										●	
Rice / Brown Rice		●								●	
Pasta		●									

Food Guide - Vitamins & Minerals

	Vitamin A Bones Best sources are from Beta-Carotene	**Vitamin B's** Production of red blood cells & new body cells, food into energy, mood, anxiety, skin, hair, hormones.	**Vitamin B6** production of progesterone, red blood cells & serotonin; low energy, depression & mood swings	**Vitamin B12** Making red blood cells & DNA, healthy nervous system, brain function & bones	**Vitamin C** Immune System, Hot Flushes, Incontinence	**Vitamin D** Bones Testosterone production.	**Vitamin E** Hot flushes Helps ease stress & depression	**Omega 3** Brain, heart, eyes, production of progesterone	**Zinc** Production of progesterone & testosterone; body's processes	**Magnesium** Hormone balance, production of progesterone & levels	**Calcium** Bones
Tofu		●								●	
Dark Chocolate									●	●	
Chard							●			●	
Dried Fruit		●	●								
Guava					●						
Kiwi Fruit					●						
Papaya					●						
Pistachio Nuts			●							●	
Trout							●	●			
Watermelon									●		
Yams									●		

Action

Become more aware of the foods you are eating and include foods in your diet from the lists above. Menopause is more about slight adjustments to your life, your pace, the foods you eat, drinks you consume, staying active and a positive mindset.

Become more active. Join an exercise class such as Yoga, Pilates, Aquafit and regular walks. Doing something physical that you enjoy, every day would be the best. Realistically I know that most ladies, myself included, would not manage that, so I aim for three times a week about three and a half hours in total of activity. Remember you are never too old to learn or have fun. But keep moving and being active. Enjoy life.

Key Learning Points

- Listen to your body. Know it's rhythm. Be in tune with it.
- Stay active, dance, run, walk, have fun. Keeping active means that you will stay more flexible. If you stay sat in a chair all day long, day after day your body will begin to seize up. Before long you will find yourself in that cycle of not being able to move around much because you don't move much. Because you don't move much, you can't move and so it goes on. If this sounds a bit like you or you are worried you're heading in that direction, take action now. Start to dance again like Beryl did in the story. BUT if you have health concerns you *MUST* consult your GP.
- Enjoy life. Don't stop having fun no matter how old you are.
- Eat fresh nutritious foods that will help your body to produce the hormones that it needs, so you feel better and can live life your way.
- Eating fresh healthy food and being active will help you to control your weight.
- Think positively. What is the best that could happen?
- Be kind to yourself.

You are doing Great

Start every day by saying something nice to yourself

Helen Breward

CHAPTER 5

Dealing with Stress

Chapter 5 - Dealing with Stress

Mavis - The Proper Cross Fairy

Long, long ago when the earth was full of magic, there was a part of the land that was ruled by fairies. This land was wondrous in all ways imaginable. It sparkled, literally sparkled with magic. It was the most intensely magical part of the earth.

Trees twinkled day and night, changing colours to suit their feelings, their emotions. Butterflies shimmered as they gracefully flapped their wings. Grass glistened and sparkled in the daylight. But it was the fairies that shone the brightest. It was the fairies that gave everything its delightful spark, sprinkling magical dust wherever they went.

Such a wonderful place to be; so peaceful, so harmonious. Everything was intertwined; everything flowed in perfect harmony, so that calm, peace and life just flowed beautifully across the land.

Now to keep this peaceful place running smoothly, the fairies themselves had to remain calm and at one with themselves, as well as each other. To do this most of them sat outside amongst the trees, the grass, the flowers, the animals, nature itself, closed their eyes, took a deep inward breath, letting it out slowly and listened to the silence, feeling the very essence of harmony as it flowed through and around all things. Spreading their arms and opening their hands they were able to feel any tiny blockages, removing them through concentrating on that spot; sending a burst of magic to that place. This they called balancing and it was vital to everything in the land.

Now, it's fair to say that no two fairies are the same. Each fairy has its own way of remaining in this state of calm. Each fairy has its own special and unique gift. Something that they are gifted at, a special talent if you like. Mavis, was different, she was not your average fairy. Mavis was extremely talented at solving problems, particularly those involving people and other fairy folk. She would often see a clear and simple solution, to what seemed like an unsolvable problem to everyone else. You see, to Mavis, problems would just unravel themselves, revealing an obvious answer, just to her. Those around her would marvel at the ease with which a solution was found, how easy things were. Problems just surrendered to her. Obviously, some problems were easier than others. Some were incredibly intricate, and some were just plain tricky. Mavis didn't care, she loved problems no matter what they were, easy, difficult or complex, she just loved solving them.

Now, because Mavis was so good, so skilled at problems, she would generally be the first one that was called. She wasn't the only fairy that solved problems; she was just simply the best. So, Mavis usually had a full caseload and she liked being busy. Going into different places of work, sorting out the issues, the problems between bosses, managers and fairy workers was exciting, thrilling and exhilarating. This is what Mavis did best; this is what she thrived on, lived for if you like. At the end of the day she would retreat to her garden, her own little private sanctuary where she could sit in nature under her favourite willow tree, next to the waterfall that flowed gently into a beautiful pond full of golden fish. This was her place of calm and peace. This was where she reconnected with nature, where she maintained her balance, her magic, her very essence.

One particular day had been busy, even more busy than usual. New cases were piling up, all marked as urgent. That was on top of the regular clients she had. Mavis suspected that 'Urgent' was being written on the paperwork, just so that she would read it first. However, too many were beginning to pop up as 'urgent' when they really weren't. This irritated her a little, but every evening she would sit in her garden and brush off all those niggles and feel the calm flowing through her again restoring her balance. After a while, Mavis began to get up a little earlier so that she could read through all the new cases, so she had the time to do everything that needed to be done. Again, after a short while Mavis began to work a little later, just 5 minutes,

"I'll just finish this first" she would say to herself.

The 'to do' list never ended, there was always something else that needed to be done. It never bothered her, she enjoyed crossing things off the list. It was satisfying.

At the end of a long, hectic week she was exhausted. Mavis felt hot and bothered, her whole body ached from the very top of her head to the tips of her toes. She was falling asleep where she stood. It was then that a decision was made that would send out ripples throughout the land, eventually causing chaos. Mavis made a split-second choice, one that on its own was not huge, but was the start of something much bigger, that would have far reaching consequences. She went straight up to bed, missing out her daily routing of sitting in the garden and restoring her balance. Before her head touched the pillow, she was fast asleep. The next morning, feeling refreshed after a good night's sleep, Mavis began to relax and enjoy the weekend. Missing one balancing session had not affected her, it was ok. Everything still flowed. Life continued as before, busy, busy, busy.

Occasionally a balancing session would be missed with no apparent affect. But... what Mavis hadn't noticed, was that her tolerance of others was not quite as good as usual. Her sleep wasn't quite as good as usual. She was suffering more and more with excessive heat, she would have hot, very hot flushes. No matter, she would catch up at the weekend, she'd sort it out then...but, then, never seemed to quite happen. And the workload grew more and more. A new habit was beginning to form; at least one balancing session was being missed every week. Now, you remember that everything was intertwined; everything flowed in perfect harmony, so that calm, peace and life flowed beautifully across the land, which is the very reason why all fairies had a daily balancing session. Slowly the natural harmony throughout the land began to falter, little blockages began to form, and people and fairies began to get on each other's nerves... More problems to solve.

It didn't take long, before Mavis didn't have the time to balance at all "One fairy won't make any difference to the flow" she thought. She began to snap at those she was helping, at clients... things were not flowing at all... As with the natural order of things, everything came to a head, the land was in total chaos. She had been called in to the crystal mine, to sort out yet another problem with the sprits, they were not following the mining guidelines and mistakes were being made. Storming into the office, Mavis snapped and flew into a rage, a huge tornado of a rage, whipping up into the mother of all storms. She was proper cross. Unfortunately, the two young girls in the office copped the lot, all her pent-up frustrations, stress and tiredness was aimed directly at them. Everything that had been steadily building over the last months just poured out. Outside, dark black clouds covered the sky, completely obliterating the sun. Thunder roared, and lightening flew across the blackness. It took two days for the storm to abate, to cool down, to feel calm again.

Once the proper cross fairy had calmed down, she realised that something had to be done. She didn't like how it had felt. The intense heat, the furnace that burned white hot from within, the anger and frustration, the sleeplessness that followed. She didn't want to go through that again.

So, off she went to see the wise fairy high up in the mountains. She would be able to help. Walking up the mountain path towards the little cottage Mavis began to feel a little better, walking briskly seemed to be helping. In front of the cottage was a babbling brook with a beautiful bridge over it. Standing on the bridge was the wise fairy, gazing into the stream. Upon reaching the bridge, the words just began to flow from Mavis. The flood gates had opened. How busy work was, how she had missed balancing sessions, the irritability, the sleeplessness, the intense heat and finally, being very ashamed of her behaviour she talked about the storm that had consumed her and how it felt afterwards.

"Have you noticed how the stream just carries on flowing? It knows where it has to go and finds a way around obstacles, but it goes at its own pace, in its own way." Asked the wise fairy, talking to no one in particular.

"You see if the stream over flows and becomes furious and raging it affects the whole of the riverbank, everything around feels the fury and is hurt in some way because of it."

"So, how do we stop the stream from becoming furious?" asked Mavis

"Look at the stream, I mean really look at it. Look into the water and see the stones that form the bottom, the foundation if you like. Each stone is supporting another. Together they are strong and firm. Now consider the role of the water plants. How they carefully intertwine themselves between and around the stones, holding them steady, providing even more support, an anchor if you like."

As Mavis studied the stream she indeed noticed those things the wise fairy had mentioned. But the longer she looked the more she spotted, the fish, the little crabs, the fresh water prawns. A small seed of peace began to grow within her. And then she took in the wider picture, how the trees and bushes, the birds and animals all relied upon the stream. But... they all had a balance, each taking and giving only what was needed, nothing more and nothing less. Calm began to descend upon her. The seed of peace grew. Mavis stayed on the bridge the rest of the day and long into the night, just looking and gaining a new understanding, a new perspective. All the time, peace growing within her. But more importantly she was getting it. How important she was, just one fairy made a big difference. She now understood how to take care of herself. Just how important, how vital it was to take time out for herself. To balance, truly balance her whole life... Things would have to change.

In the morning the wise fairy brought Mavis a nice hot cup of tea.

Turning to her, Mavis said "I have never felt this peaceful. I get it now. I understand the true meaning of balance. It's not just something we are told to do. I get it. Really get it."

From out of a pocket, the wise fairy produced a clear crystal ball. Hovering it in front of Mavis, she said

"Pour all that peace into the ball. Every last drop, it may be a colour, your favourite colour. Just watch it swirling around as you pour it all in there... Now, pour in all the balance you have gained. Notice the colour, another favourite, how it swirls around the peace. Finally pour in all the calmness you feel, every last drop. Watch how all the colours intertwine, swirl around each other. This is your very own ball of peace, calm and balance, feel the peace and calm emanating from it, notice the vibration, warmth or tingle of balance. With your eyes closed I want you to find a place within your body to let the ball live. Somewhere where it will be comfortable and grow, somewhere you are happy with it living."

It felt good to have her own personal ball of peace, calm and balance. Something she could draw upon.

“But what do I do if I feel the storm begin to build, I don’t want it to rage again like before?” Mavis asked with eyes full of worry.

“Do you remember how it felt when you walked up the mountain to get here? A little exercise, a brisk walk often takes the energy out of a storm you know. Taking in good nutritious food and water will help the plants, bushes and trees to be healthy and strong. Remember a solid foundation is essential.” Replied the wise fairy with tenderness.

So, from that day forward, from that moment onwards Mavis never missed a balancing session. She never allowed the storm to build, always removing the energy with a brisk walk. But just as importantly she got other fairies to help her. She made changes to her life, so she wasn’t so busy, so she had time for herself and those things that were important to her life. Those things that made her happy and complete. Balance was perfect. Harmony was restored throughout the land.

Information

This time out is very important, very beneficial to everyone, no matter the age. Stress affects us all young and old. Meditation is just one powerful way of dealing and coping with life.

Stress is one of the big causes of hot flushes in menopause. Keeping control of it will help enormously. Stress also reduces progesterone production, as resources are used to produce more cortisol, the main stress hormone instead. Therefore, levels of progesterone become depleted. Remembering that progesterone is our natural anti-depressant and anti-anxiety hormone, you can clearly see the effect that this will have on you. So, reducing stress levels is generally a must for everyone, but relating to menopause it is even more imperative. It's about finding a slightly different rhythm, adjusting your pace of life; in essence taking care of yourself, putting you first.

Other ways of dealing with stress are:

- A daily meditation is a powerful tool.
- Listening to hypnosis recordings.
  Download your free hypnosis recording with this book from www.helenbreward.com/menopause-my-way
- Practise the breathing exercise in chapter 1.
- Taking regular exercise. This does not have to be running, weight lifting or any activity that fills you with dread. In my opinion, it does have to be something or several something's that you enjoy because you will benefit more from it and it will be much more

sustainable in the long run, which is what you are ultimately aiming to do.

- Cutting down on the caffeine drinks i.e. coffee, tea & fizzy drinks
- Eating healthily, foods with lower refined sugar content (see food list for help). Foods which contain vitamin C and B6 are particularly good for stress.
- Drinking plenty of water, ice water is great.
- Reducing some of the things that you can, that are not so important or urgent. Ask others to help you.
- Getting a good night's sleep.
- Making yourself a priority because you are important. You cannot take care of others nor do your job well indefinitely if you don't take care of yourself. So, looking after you benefits those around you.
- Leaving work at work. Putting clear boundaries in place for yourself, so that work does not carry on after hours, weekends and even during holidays. Switching off.
- Spending time with your loved ones and doing things that are important to you, which have real meaning to your quality of life is essential to your mental and physical wellbeing.

Activity

Spend 5-10 minutes meditating or even just sitting in the silence every day. You may find that first thing in the morning sets you up for the day ahead or in the evening helps you to decompress. Whatever helps you best is what matters. If you have not tried meditation before, or are not sure how to practice it, here's another story to help you.

It was a cold miserable day, the clouds were dark and grey, and even the birds were staying away, not even singing. This kind of day can lower your mood if you let it. And so, it was with my eldest granddaughter, Melissa. She popped in to see me after school. I can always tell when she has something on her mind, today was no exception.

With a drink in hand and a snack by her side, I wait for Melissa to take that long deep breath, that sigh that tells me she is ready to let go. One simple question is all it takes.

"How was your day love?"

Looking at her, I see the floodgates open, releasing frustration, confusion, tensions, but most of all I understand that she is struggling to make sense of all her emotions.

"Grandma, I find it hard to cope with everything sometimes. I have a lot of homework, Lucy always wants me to help her or to play, which I love to do and how can I say no to her, she's my little sister. Mum needs help too around the house and with the pets. There's so much to do and I have a big test next week that I have to study for."

A big sigh leaves her body as tears begin to roll down her face.

"And I fell out with Sue my best friend."

"That sounds like a lot of stress to me, a lot to cope with."

Another big sigh leaves Melissa's body. Looking as if she has the weight of the world on her shoulders, Melissa talks about the argument with Sue. Eventually, she realises that 'sorry' is the answer.

"Would you like to know how I deal with stress?" nodding her head, I continue

"How about I teach you how to meditate? Once you know how to do it and practise it every day even if it's only for 5 or 10 minutes, you will feel much better. This is a skill for the rest of your life Melissa."

Explaining that I'll talk for a little while, asking her to see or feel things in her mind, in that darkness behind the eyelids; then we will sit in the silence for a while.

We begin by taking in a deep breath, a cleansing breath, letting out all that pent-up stress and tension from the day. With eyes closed, I begin to guide Melissa through the wonders of meditation.

"Breathe in a pure white light, feel yourself filling up with it, as I surround us both with the white light of love and protection. We ask our guides to help us on our journey today.

Now picture yourself in a meadow, a lovely warm summer's day. You can feel the sun on your face, the grass beneath your feet. It's so peaceful. Just breathe. If you should find your mind wandering, just focus on breathing that inward breath, that outward breath.

Let's go for a walk in the meadow, along a little path that leads you down the side of a stream. As you watch the water for a time, you can see the fish swimming, the water plants waving in the gentle current, the multitude of stones on the bottom of the stream, each one different and interesting. You feel even calmer than you did before as you just watch the stream gently flowing along.

Up ahead you can see the wise old apple tree, I want you to just sit under it for a time, absorb the wisdom and understanding you need right now, this very moment. That understanding will come to you in ways that are just right for you. It might be a thought, feeling or even pictures, but it will be right for you.

Now continue, through the gate and up the mountain path. As you walk up the path there may be others walking with you. You are joined by an animal that is there to help you, to be with you, to guide you in some way.

At the top of the mountain, you look down on the Indian encampment and the river below. Take yourself now down to the river, where you will find some big leaves on the ground. Make a wish or several wishes on the leaves, and then you can place them on the water and watch the river take them away.

Now, walk over to the campfire and sitting down, look into the flames as we go into the silence."

This time the silence lasts about 5 minutes, which is a long time for a beginner, a first time.

"Now, I want you to ask your guide for a gift for yourself to bring back with you.

When you are ready you can open your eyes."

Looking at my granddaughter, I see peace and calm. I'm so proud of her. She excitedly tells me about her first meditation, the colours she could see, how she struggled to find the wise old apple tree, but somehow just knew it was there. The little black and white rabbit that was her guide that stayed with her to the end, giving her a gift, a beautiful seashell. With practice she will see and experience so much more.

The following day, Melissa reported that she had had a great night's sleep and wanted to do it again after school. Best of all, she was friends again with Sue and she was sorting out times to do her homework, help mum and play with Lucy. The huge mountain of problems from the previous day had now been reduced to a small manageable pile.

Before long, meditation became our daily routine. Over time our twosome, became a threesome, then a foursome as others joined in. How perfect is that?

Take time out for yourself

You are worth it

Helen Breward

Key Learning Points

Stress is known as a hormone stealer because the body diverts resources away from the production of certain hormones, like progesterone to make cortisol the main stress hormone.

- Find ways that suit you to de-stress at the end of the day, meaning, do something very physical to burn up the cortisol or the opposite, deep relaxation, which releases hormones that combat the chemical effects of stress.
- Chat with a friend, get 'it' off your chest.
- Learn to meditate. This is a very powerful method for stress management.
- Stress is a very big trigger for hot flushes. So, managing this will help you to be cooler and may also relieve other symptoms like anxiety and panic.
- Download the free hypnosis recording from: www.helenbreward.com/menopause-my-way
- Listen to your recording every day if possible. Find half an hour to comfortably sit back with your eyes closed, where you won't be disturbed.
- Be active, have fun.
- Cut down on caffeine drinks like tea, coffee and fizzy drinks.
- Drink plenty of cold water, stay hydrated.

- Share the load. Get others to help you wherever possible.
- Put clear work boundaries in place, so that you 'switch off'
- Spend time with your loved ones. Those people that give true meaning to your life.

You are Important
You Matter

Helen Breward

CHAPTER 6

Sex!

Chapter 6 - SEX!

What's that I hear you cry! That's the thing we used to do when we were so much younger and had no children. The thing we thought we invented. How that makes me smile now. Sex is like everything, a skill. The more you practise the better you get, or more accurately, you get to know your own body, your likes and dislikes. What turns you on.

Somewhere along the way, amongst the chaos of life sex drive, especially in women, seems to drive off. I suppose the question is will it ever return?

Many years ago, in a village not far from here there lived a beautiful young lady who fell in love with a handsome fellow from a neighbouring town. They spent many hours talking and getting to know each other. Giggling at silly jokes, remembering childhood escapades and dreaming of the future. Life was full of hope and promise for the young couple.

Eventually, they decided to follow their dream and start their biggest adventure together, a road trip. One that would lead them across the world, to a place they didn't even know existed.

As they set off full of hope and excitement everything was amazing, they spent lots of time together, doing little things for the other that said 'I love you". Little pats on the behind, a smile, a tender touch of the hand, a stroke of the back, you get what I mean. And those frequent moments, when two became one, were just pure raw unconditional love, the kind of thing that makes your heart skip several beats, a choir of angels sing out loud for the whole world to hear. Pure exquisite joy.

For quite a while the journey was great fun. Occasionally, there was a bump in the road or the scenery wasn't quite so pleasant, but they carried on driving and these things passed.

One day they were joined by a very small passenger, one that would change their whole trip. The small one was very demanding, needing lots of attention and screamed out loud if it didn't get what it needed. That sounds like a poor deal I hear you say. But, now here's the thing, the small one comes with big promises and huge amounts of love and joy. Holding the little one and soothing its cries became the most important thing to do. And nothing could beat holding the sleeping passenger. It's that deep feeling of peace and contentment. I suppose the outcome was tiredness, and the casualty was those less and less frequent moments when they became one. Still, the journey was fun and so enjoyable, as the trip took in different destinations to those imagined at the beginning. Everything was good.

Very slowly, almost unnoticeably some little things began to get forgotten, like the pat on the behind, that tender touch, spending time together on their own, doing some of the things they used to before the passenger came along. I guess they were too tired and had no energy. Despite this, his passion and drive was still as strong as ever and focused on the road. However, hers had driven off in another direction, stopped by the side of the road ages ago or driven completely off into the desert, never to be seen again. This began to cause friction between them.

Stopping in a beautiful village one day, she began talking to a friendly shopkeeper, who told tales of a wise woman who lived in the forest just beyond the boundaries. Ummm, she thought I wonder if she could help me? On her own, she found the path that led to the boundaries of the village. Taking a deep breath, she stepped over the line and carried on into the forest. Along the way, she noticed all the lush greenery, the different shades, shapes and smells of the forest. The deeper she went the more she noticed, the calmer she felt.

Eventually, a little cottage appeared in a clearing. Pausing for a second to take a deep breath, she then gathered up her courage to knock on the door. But, before her hand touched the door, a voice from behind said

"Hello, I've been waiting for you. Come, sit down and have a cup of tea." Said the wise woman with a gentle knowing smile.

She could instantly see why this was the wise woman. Before long the tea had worked its magic and the whole tale of the road trip and its passenger unfolded, how her drive and passion had driven off into the desert. And her worst fear revealed. She wanted another passenger to fill the car, to make the journey complete. But, she also knew, or thought she did, that those intimate moments were few and far between now, so what would it be like with another passenger? Tears rolled down her face as the weight of worry fell away, just through saying it out loud.

"Sometimes, when we take on passengers our reserves get depleted, but we don't always listen to the purr of the engine. We don't always put in the best lubricant and fuel. Sometimes, we take shortcuts and use the cheapest substitutes we can find. This may be ok for a quick fix in an emergency, but over time performance will suffer as the engine doesn't have what it needs to give its all like it did in the beginning" replied the wise woman, full of compassion and understanding. Continuing she added:

"How often do you clean the car? When do you treat it to a tender, loving polish, really show it that it's important, that you love it? Can you remember the last time both of you went out together alone?"

Dismay, crept across the younger woman's face, as she realised how things had changed without her noticing. She felt like a complete failure. Putting her arms around her the wise woman spoke of this as part of her journey in becoming a wise woman.

Wandering now together, through the forest the older began to show and teach the younger just which fruits and vegetables would help her to bring back that passion. How to gently caress the leaves, just the right amount of water here and there. How to speak softly to each plant, to gently encourage leaves to unfold, flowers to bloom and fruit to ripen.

But, the biggest lesson of all was learning how to be her again. Finding herself. Somehow, she had been lost in the needs of others along the journey. Now, she was learning that she was important, to take time out to just be, to breathe, to recharge, to be beautiful again.

Before long, it was time to go and re-join the road trip. As they said their goodbye's the wise one had one last piece of wisdom to impart.

"Remember what you have learned. As your journey continues your engine will require alterations to the lubricants and fuel you put in as it becomes a little older. The way you look after it will also subtly change. Listen to its purr, to its very heartbeat. Always be in tune with your car and it will serve you well, making the journey so much more fun and exciting."

Placing a pearl of wisdom around the younger woman's neck, the older lady smiled and waved goodbye as she, the younger but wiser woman left the forest to carry on her journey.

Smile

Laugh

have Fun

be Passionate

Enjoy the Journey

Helen Breward

Information

Just because you are going through menopause or 'that age'; did I mention how I really hate that phrase? It doesn't mean that is the end of sex. It means you are now freer to be spontaneous, no interruptions as the children, if you have them, have either left home or adult enough to be taking care of themselves and finding their own lives.

Yes, as you get older sex may change a bit, but you can still really enjoy it, it is good for you on many different levels.

- Strengthens the intimate bond between a couple.
- The brain releases oxytocin 'love hormone' and endorphins before orgasm is reached. These hormones are also natural painkillers.
- Sex reduces stress levels.
- Boosts your immune system.
- Helps you to feel relaxed afterwards, the afterglow.
- Keeps you supple, it is still being active, so in my book is a form of exercise!
- Feel young, you are only as old as you think you are. Sex is believed to be a great anti-ageing activity. So, plenty of sex then!

Some women find that their sex drive or libido takes a nosedive around this time of their lives. It can sometimes happen when children come along too. Practically speaking this may be due to an oestrogen & progesterone imbalance or low testosterone levels. However, with women of childbearing age, it may also be a bit more complex, especially if childbirth has been a traumatic experience, in the form of subconsciously avoiding sex so you don't have any more children. These issues can be quite deep for some ladies and may require help to overcome. My advice as always to these women is to seek medical help.

Back to the menopause. Low libido levels are more likely to be because of the drop-in oestrogen, progesterone and testosterone. One practical thing you can do, as I have mentioned before is to make sure you eat those foods that will provide your body with the nutrients that it needs to make the hormones. It's a bit like making a cake, you know you want to make a lovely moist chocolate cake and know the exact ingredients necessary to produce the perfect results. However, looking through your cupboards you only have a few of the ingredients, but you still try to make the cake. You have done your best with the resources available, but it's nowhere near the perfect moist chocolate cake you wanted or dreamed of. So, as you pop it in your mouth, you don't get that same enjoyment, that same sensation on your tongue. You feel disappointed, a bit low in mood because of it and don't feel like being intimate that night.

Now, imagine that same scenario, you open your cupboard, realise you don't have all the ingredients and don't want to settle for anything less than that lovely moist chocolate cake. So, and this is what makes a world of difference, you nip out to the shop and get those missing ingredients. So, now as you carefully and lovingly bake that cake, your anticipation builds as you stir and mix everything together in just the right amounts. You can smell it as it bakes in the oven. The aroma building expectations higher and higher. The timer rings, out of the oven it comes, looking so delicious and perfect. Sitting down with a cup of tea, you take that first bite. A million sensations spring into life. First, you notice how lovely and moist it is, perfect. Then you relish the chocolatey flavour as it dances on your tongue, quickly followed by a whole host of other delicate sensations as each one of the ingredients release their essence, their, zest, their sweetness. You have a wonderful party going on in your mouth. You feel excited, uplifted and great. Intimacy is definitely on the cards.

See the food charts Chapter 4

Menopause is about tweaking your lifestyle, finding this new and liberated you. This also includes your sex life. You may have to develop a few adjustments along the way.

For some, it may take longer to feel aroused and experience an orgasm. There are plenty of ways to enhance the experience –

- Take time, don't rush. After all, you don't have the threat of a possible interruption.
- Why not have a lovely bath or shower together. Light some candles, set the scene. Being practical, you are killing two birds with one stone as they say; having fun and getting clean!
- Undress each other. When did you last do that?
- Feed each other, this can be a very sensual experience.

- Gently stroke your partners skin.
- Remember how passionately you used to kiss? Bring back that same passion.
- Don't be afraid to try out new things.

This is by no means a comprehensive list, just a few simple ideas.

Vaginal Dryness and other conditions

Some women may find intercourse painful and uncomfortable during and after menopause. One of the possible reasons for this is again lower oestrogen levels, which could reduce blood flow to the vagina and less natural lubrication. It's a bit like trying to slide on a path with trainers on. For a great slide you need lubrication like oil or grease, so the two surfaces pass easily over each other. One way of keeping the blood flowing to the vaginal area is to keep using it, in other words, keep engaging in foreplay and sex. It's that old saying 'use it or lose it'. Sexual arousal increases blood flow to the tissues surrounding the vaginal area. Then, because of the increase in blood pressure in those tissues, moisture from the blood vessels and spongy tissues flows into the glands surrounding the entrance of the vagina. The glands then release their natural lubricant around the opening of the vagina.

You can obtain lubricants from the chemist, pharmacy or your Doctor. A warm bath and soap-free cleansers are also reported to be helpful in relieving symptoms.

Another condition, which can sometimes be linked to

vaginal dryness is the thinning of the vaginal wall. This is also due to lower oestrogen levels.

A condition known as vaginismus, which is the vaginal muscles contracting involuntarily can make sex painful. If something hurts or is painful we are less likely to want to repeat the experience.

Genital infections and tumours are also other possible reasons for bleeding and pain during sex. My advice if you are experiencing pain and/or bleeding during intercourse then see your GP as soon as you can.

Why sex is better after menopause

- No worries about getting pregnant. No periods, no tampons, no pads, no worries about excessive bleeding, no birth control needed. Feel the FREEDOM this gives you.
- Your children are likely to be young adults and independent, so not likely to interrupt you or need attention in the middle of the night. Which generally means you sleep better.
- More time for yourself and your partner. You can rediscover you again. Do things you both want to do and enjoy, rather than what the kids want or will keep them occupied.
- Be comfortable with who you are. For a lot of women, menopause is a time of liberation, a time to redefine themselves, rekindle old passions that were put aside long ago.

- Enjoyment of sexual freedom as you realise you are still sexy and desirable.
- Usually, financially secure.
- A clear and secure career path.

What I'm saying is enjoy a good healthy sex life after menopause, it's good for you.

Action

Eat healthy as previously mentioned. By doing this you are tipping the scales in your favour and helping your body to make and do what it needs to do. Be adventurous, wear something that makes you feel special & sexy. You are an exceptional lady, so treat yourself that way. Have FUN and ENJOY SEX.

Key Learning Points

- Put into your body, every day, those essential ingredients that it needs to make the necessary hormones, oestrogen, progesterone & testosterone; Omega 3, Vitamins C, D & E, Zinc, Magnesium & B6 see food charts for specific foods. If you don't have any lemons, you can't make lemonade.
- Take time out for you and your partner. Rekindle some of those old passions & pleasures that somehow were left behind during those child-rearing years.
- Find out who you are. Be comfortable with you.
- Don't be afraid to seek medical help.
- Take more time for foreplay, this will help your body to produce its natural lubricant. Sometimes things take a little longer as we get older.
- If you need to use additional lubrication to enjoy sex, you can obtain it from a pharmacy or your Doctor. Don't let uncomfortable intercourse put you off being intimate with your loved one. Do something about it.
- Relax and HAVE FUN

You

are an

Amazing

Goddess

full of

Wisdom

Helen Breward

CHAPTER 7

Living with a hot partner

Chapter 7 - Living with a hot partner

Living with a hot partner can be bloody frustrating, I'm learning to be so patient. But god the mood swings, I never know if sweet Sally-Ann is going to walk through the door or the exorcist. I pray for Sally-Ann. Sometimes she is there. Wistfully remembering those times gone by when we were both so young. I can hear her laughter now, that amazing laugh that just makes my heart sing, the laugh that tells me so much, that life is great, the love between us is stronger than ever. How she lights up a room with just a smile. My world, my everything.

When we were younger, there were stories of 'That time of life', but we didn't take much notice, after all, it was so far in the future. I'm pretty sure we thought those stories were exaggerated. All of a sudden, we are here, where did the years go? I guess we were too busy raising a family, working and living life to notice the years rolling by.

Now life has changed again as it inevitably does. We are back to just the two of us, well most of the time. We are lucky enough to have regular visits from our grown-up children and grandchildren, family and friends. So yes, we are blessed. But... there are those times when my patience is truly tested. Being positive, those are the times when she helps me to become a better partner. She helps me a lot!

Bedtime, a time to snuggle under the covers all warm and cosy. A time to rest and recharge. The bedroom is freezing, I pull on my woolly socks and thermal pyjamas, as she does a whole covers on and covers off thing all night. My heart goes out to her as she drips like a tap, burns like the hottest of furnaces, loses sleep and feels so tired in the morning. The bedclothes are soaking, and she won't let me help. She's so annoyed with herself... or is it me that's upset her? Have I forgotten to do something or temporarily lost my mind reading skills? I hold my tongue.

There are many days when I wonder how on earth she has the strength to get through the day, especially when it's been a tough night. But, painting a smile on her face, she goes off to work. Those are the days I try to help by cooking the evening meal. One less thing for her to do. In all honesty, it doesn't always happen as much as I would like. It depends greatly on who walks in the door first. Knowing how irritable we all can get when we are tired, those are the nights that can be the most challenging, when she feels the weight of the world on her shoulders.

I know she's sad at this change. I know she gets confused and wonders why? I know she loves to hold a bundle of joy in her arms, those days are over... in her mind. I tell her grandchildren will come and fill her heart with joy again. But I see the sadness in her eyes. I feel so helpless.

She feels fat and ugly, not the beautiful temptress she used to be. But to me, she is still the goddess that stole my heart, gave me so much love, laughter and joy. She is simply the world to me.

It doesn't matter that she shouts at me. It doesn't matter that she's hot and cold, hot and cold. It doesn't matter how moody, irrational or anxious she gets, I love her, and we will get through this. I will have my Sally-Ann back one day.

You see I'm there to catch her if she stumbles, or falls, walking right by her side, day and night. Silently I put my arms around her, hold her close, and hold her tight, while she sobs. She doesn't know why the tears are flowing, they just are. There seems to be no rhyme or reason, just what is now. And now we have tears. I try hard to get it, to not fix her. That's so hard, I just want to make her better, to fix what's wrong, what's broken. That's what men do, fix things, make the broken work again. Going against all my programming, my instincts to make her better, to take the pain away, I just hold her tight let the tears flow but most of all say nothing. It just feels wrong to me... but it's not about me, so I've learned. It's what she needs, what works for her. Even in this maelstrom of emotion and change, she's still teaching me, showing me another way to be. Slowly, slowly I'm getting it, how to fix her. Not with a spanner, hammer or a spade... but with silence, with a hug, with love, with patience... Oh, so much patience. To let the tears fall unchecked, that's the hardest. But once the flood subsides, calmness descends. Slowly, very slowly the clouds disappear and the sun begins to shine again. A weight has been lifted and that familiar, beautiful heart-stopping smile spreads across her face. And the pain is gone, forgotten. She is fixed... for now. And that's good enough for me.

Despite all of that she's positive and upbeat, most of the time, finding a new her, a new way to be... or is she just rediscovering what she once was before the role of mum? Only better, more confident and wiser. I watch as she flexes her wings, spreads them and prepares to fly. I'm filled with pride, joy and hope. Fly as high as you can. Now is my turn to step back, to take care of the little stuff.

Life is taking on a new quality, one of new adventures, joy, laughter and playfulness. Watching as she opens her arms and embraces it all with confidence, a new-found confidence that grows every day. I see how easily she encompasses many different roles, switching in a heartbeat, with a big smile. Turning to me she grabs my hand, pulling me. Together we run toward the next adventure, laughing and smiling. Now is a golden time. Life is good.

Patience is a virtue
Stretched tight like a rubber band

Colin Breward

Someone's other half!

Information - Male Menopause?

This is a debatable question, that has been discussed for decades. According to the NHS, the male hormone testosterone declines steadily from around the age of 30/40 by a small percentage each year, which they believe is unlikely to cause problems.

However, around the end of the 40's and early 50's some men experience symptoms similar to women going through the menopause.

- Irritability
- Mood swings
- Lack of sleep
- Tiredness
- Short-term memory & poor concentration problems
- Low energy
- Lack of enthusiasm
- Development of a larger stomach area or 'man boobs'
- Reduced muscle mass
- Low libido
- Erectile dysfunction

These symptoms can affect the individual's enjoyment of life. Whilst many may attribute this to male menopause, there are other things that need to be explored like lifestyle, diet, stress, anxiety, too much alcohol, not enough exercise, smoking, poor or lack of sleep as these issues can also be the cause of the above symptoms.

Working with a lot of stressed clients, I see quite a few of the above issues, irritability, mood swings, lack of sleep, tiredness, poor concentration, foggy brain, low energy, lack of enthusiasm, low libido & erectile dysfunction.

Learning to manage stress better has, in my experience, helped every one of those symptoms. The advice, as always is if you are concerned about your health, visit your Doctor.

https://www.nhs.uk/conditions/male-menopause/

Action

Just remember your support is vital. You are doing a great job just by being there. Look after yourself, eat healthily, exercise and take a few minutes out of each day for yourself. These menopause moments will end.

Key Learning Points

- It can be challenging living with a partner who is going through the menopause.
- The key to 'fixing' women is with a hug, an ear and silence.
- When women cry, it's often a good thing. It's one of the ways we let go of emotions, that and talking.
- Saying things out loud helps you to make sense of it because you actually hear it, not just think it.
- Patience is needed in great quantities sometimes.
- During this phase of life, helping each other with everyday things will just make life a little easier.
- Underneath it all your partner is still the beautiful lady you fell in love with.
- These menopause moments will not last forever.
- Managing your stress levels will help a lot of the common symptoms.
- Men may also experience similar symptoms as their hormone levels change.
- Support each other. This is a golden time, a time to be enjoyed.

Always Remember You are Amazing

Helen Breward

CHAPTER 8

After the heat has gone

Chapter 8 - After the heat has gone

As I wander slowly through my garden today, I notice those long hot summer days have cooled down to a gentle warmth, like a soft comfortable blanket, just perfect. I reach out and touch the soft delicate flowers, feeling the silky petals in my hand, taking in the beautiful vivid colours in all its splendour.

As it is with autumn, the garden changes, the colours of summer fade, as the richness of gold, orange and red shines through, adding another dimension to this wonderful peaceful place. I notice my hands are a little more wrinkled as they reach out and touch the golden leaves. The grass is still there to be sat on, played on, enjoyed. Behind me I hear giggles of laughter as the children and grandchildren follow me, playing games, having such fun. Small chubby arms are thrown around my neck. My heart fills and swells with love.

I'm transported back to a time which seems so long ago now. A whole other lifetime, when my children were little and my mum looked on with such a beautiful, loving smile. A feeling like no other in the world. There are many times when I wish that feeling could be bottled, joking that the world's problems could be solved with its contents. There's a part of me that is not joking.

There is so much to be grateful for. Yes, there are days which seem a struggle to find any little thing to be thankful for, but those are the times when we need to remember the little things, like a smile from a passing stranger, a convenient parking space or noticing a flower growing up through the concrete path. You see, the way we think affects our world and our physical bodies. Thinking negatively affects the physical body as well as the mind. So, on those tough days, it's more important than ever to look for the small things to be grateful for. After all, the small things are often what matters the most.

With age comes wisdom, so they say. But, I think it's a whole lot more than that. As I stand back and watch my family growing up, I reflect on my own life journey, on the very quiet, shy young girl I once was who wouldn't say boo to a goose, whose voice was hardly heard. A big smile creeps across my face. Wisdom is not just knowing how to cook different food, how to treat a bump or a cut or know the names of plants and trees, but it's much deeper; a deeper level of knowing, a sense or a feeling, empowerment. This is the very time of a woman's life when for some, that deeper sense, that feeling of empowerment is lost like a ship drifting aimlessly on the ocean. The birds have flown the nest, the body is creaking more, some see it as the beginning of the end. And I guess this is where, for me, the true meaning of wisdom comes in. You see you have a choice, there is always a choice. You can take the view of 'The end is nigh', 'The best years of my life have gone', 'Downhill from now on' or you can see it as a new beginning, time for you to really shine even brighter than before. This is your time now, you have given so much to all those around you for so long. NOW, it's your time, your turn. What do you want this next Chapter of your story to say? If your life story was a play, how would it look? What would the actors be doing & saying? Allow yourself to just dream away. So, my question is, what will you change? What will you do next for yourself, your own dreams, your own play?

Watching my girls, wondering where their journey will take them with a sense of pride. I know they are already wiser than they realise, stronger and more capable than they can ever dream of. My hope is to guide them to find their own deeper sense of wisdom and empowerment, to be strong and courageous, to take life by the horns and run with it to the very end. Life is for living.

The sound of "Grandma" brings me back from reflecting. What could be better than the picture of my girls smiling faces looking at me? Absolutely nothing, this moment is perfect.

We are soon joined by the men in our lives, that just completes the picture. In their own way, they are also wise. I laugh. Wise enough to know when to talk, when to stop talking and most importantly when a hug is all that is needed. The difficulty is that men have that need to fix what is broken. Women don't usually want to be fixed, more often than not, they just want to be hugged or listened to. Women are such complex creatures because we care about everything, because we care for everyone, because we feel so deeply. Even we don't always understand ourselves. It seems to me, on occasions, that men don't stand a chance. Only the wisest, who know all this and learn the ebb and flow of their woman's emotions are able to sail the sea of relationship with success. It can often be a stormy sea, but storms blow out and lead to calmer waters, pleasant destinations and wonderful experiences.

By my side is the man that has helped me through so much of life's challenges, he walks, strong and firm, always there. We share a smile that says so much more than 'I'm having fun.' A new path appears in the garden. New places to see. New wonders to experience. New discoveries to be made. Just the feeling, just the sense of adventure and discovery fills me with anticipation and excitement. Some may take me far away from home. Others may be right on my doorstep. Life is full of surprises. Life is an adventure. So, with eyes open wide, to possibilities and opportunities, we glance at each other and go hand in hand on this adventure, wherever it takes us. Together.

Do what you Dream of Have an Amazing Life

Helen Breward

Information

The way we think affects the body on a physical level. Negative thinking, not only makes life feel a struggle, tough and joyless, but it also transcends into the physical body. We have less physical resistance.

Try out this demonstration that will show you the connection between mind and body.

- Find a partner.
- Put your arms out in front of you, a bit like a zombie pose!
- Then the partner just presses down gently on your arms to show your normal resistance
- Next, still with your arms outstretched, think of the absolute worst thing that has ever happened or could happen to you. In other words, think negatively.
- Again, get your partner to press down on your arms. You should notice that they are easier to push down. Less resistance.
- Finally, repeat the exercise, but thinking about the best, most awesome thing that has ever happened or could happen to you.
- Lastly, get your partner to press down on your arms. You should notice that there is more resistance. Not so easy to push down.

Swap over and repeat the whole exercise with your partner. You push down on their arms.

Your whole attitude to this phase of life is key. You can choose just how you are going to handle it, mentally and physically. Just a few adjustments here and there will make a lot of difference to you and your symptoms. There are a lot of positives in your life, I'm sure. Welcome each day with a smile. Embrace the changes. But most of all…

ENJOY YOUR LIFE, YOUR WAY.

Action

Do something new. It doesn't have to be a big huge thing like moving to another country. It can be something as simple as trying a different type of coffee or hot chocolate in the local coffee shop. It could be taking a course and learning something new. Something you have wanted to do for a long time, but never gotten around to. It could be walking in a place you have never been before. It doesn't matter, just do something new. Make a pledge to yourself to do this every day, every week, every month. Whatever suits you. Do it for yourself. This is your time now.

Key Learning Points

- Embrace life
- Do something new, something exciting, something you have always wanted to do.
- Your positive attitude is key.
- Do the mind-body connection exercise to understand and feel the impact of your thoughts on your body.
- Thinking positively will affect your feelings, which will affect your physical body.
- Change those negative thoughts to positive ones.
- Make a few adjustments to your life here and there.
- Feel that sense of adventure. Go on an adventure.
- Start each day with a smile and ENJOY YOUR LIFE, YOUR WAY.

Life is like a River,

You can Stand on the Bank and Watch

Or

Jump in and Enjoy the Ride

Helen Breward

My Top 10 Tips
For
Managing
Menopause

Top Tip 1 – Know your own Triggers

I've lost count of the times ladies have sat in my consulting room and assured me that there are no triggers. So, I wait for that light bulb moment that invariably comes, usually several weeks later. You see, part of it is recognising those things that trigger a hot flush. To help you become more aware, I have compiled a list of 10 common triggers and their quick fixes below: -

1. Stress and/or anxiety.

Stress is known as a hormone stealer. Long term it can be damaging to the body. Your immune system and progesterone levels will suffer from stress, as nutrients are diverted away from their production to make cortisol the main stress hormone. After all, your body is preparing to run away or stand up and have a fight. Its main job is your survival. The Breathing in Chapter 1 is great to reduce stress & anxiety. Listen to the free hypnosis recording with this book www.helenbreward.com/menopause-my-way.

2. Hot and Hot together e.g. a hot drink and a hot meal; cooking in a hot room.

Have a cold drink with a hot meal. Remove one of the hot things. If cooking in a hot room is a problem, have a nice glass of ice cold water to hand.

3. Too many clothes, covers, wrapped up too much.

Wear layers of thinner clothes so you can take some off if you need to. Materials like cotton that allow your skin to breathe and a very light chiffon are good to wear. Lighter tog duvets are also very helpful at night time. One issue here could be partners who require a heavier duvet. The answer is to use single duvets, one each.

4. Enclosed spaces.

This can also trigger anxiety and panic. Open doors or windows.

Belly Breathing as described in Chapter 1. Sit or stand by a window. The light will help you to feel as if you are in an open, bigger space, less enclosed. In your mind, you have all the space you need.

5. Tiredness.

Early/sensible bedtime. Burning the candle at both ends, generally maybe okay if a one-off. But repeatedly, in all likelihood will not be so good for you. Your mind and body need rest. Reduce stimulation in the hour before bedtime e.g. no screens or caffeine drinks. Allow a short time to de-stress and begin to unwind.

6. Low sugar – hunger.

This is not an excuse to overeat, rather eating three regular meals a day, making sure you eat enough protein with each meal and plenty of foods that contain those vitamins and minerals that help support the body in menopause. Some night sweats may be due to low sugar levels at night, especially if you have missed meals or have irregular eating patterns. Try having something small and healthy about an hour before bed e.g. piece of fruit.

7. Red wine, white wine and alcohol

Grape-based alcohol and other alcoholic drinks can be triggers for some ladies. Avoid wine/alcohol. If you do drink it, you do so with the knowledge that you could have a hot flush as a result. My ladies often say that it is these alcoholic induced hot flushes, night sweats in particular, that are the hottest and worst ones of all.

8. Strong emotions e.g. stress & anger

The body is flooded with stress hormones, so they need to be burned off by doing a physical activity and/or deep relaxation, meditation. The breathing technique in Chapter 1, taking time out for yourself. The longer I work with this issue, the more I understand just how emotion-based menopause and hot flushes are. Again, proving how strong the mind-body connection is. See Top Tip 5 for an excellent exercise to demonstrate this.

9. Rushing around, busy lifestyle/diary.

Re-organise your diary/lifestyle as much as you can to enable a slower pace wherever possible. Slow down just a bit, especially in the supermarket. Breathe. It is about a slight change in pace.

10. Dehydration.

Drink plenty of water. It is recommended that we drink about 2 litres of fluid a day. That does not include caffeinated drinks like tea, coffee, fizzy drinks or alcohol. These are likely to dehydrate you. Keep a bottle of water with you.

Top Tip 2 -The simple things can make life easier

I guess here, I'm talking about general things you can do to make your life easier.

Quite often it is about planning ahead, for example writing out a weekly dinner menu, so that it takes all the thinking out of dinner time at the end of a busy day. Doing this also makes your food shopping easier.

Do the shopping with your partner, friend or family member, they can help with the packing and a chat as you push the trolley around.

If you know you are going to be late home from work or are on a late shift, prepare a meal in advance. This will stop you just grabbing the nearest processed microwave meal. Let's be honest here, I've fallen into that category many, many times and had the waistline and the spotty skin to prove it. Now, I'm converted to fresh is best, as much as possible.

Prepare your lunch for work the night before. Doing that will allow for a calmer more relaxed breakfast, with one less thing to do before you disappear out of the door.

Don't pressure yourself to be perfect. Ask yourself, how much does it really matter in the great scheme of things, if you don't manage to scrub the house from top to bottom today? Will the world come to a stop if you don't clean? I'm not being flip here, just giving you a sense of perspective. You don't have to do everything all in one go. Spread things out, pace yourself.

Ask for help. Delegate wherever possible. Let others help you. If you can, get someone else to do the tasks you either don't want to do or find difficult.

Organise your diary. Write in when you are working, personal appointments and anything else you need to do. I use different coloured highlighters for clients, writing, personal stuff and meetings. This really does help take the pressure off and keep me organised.

Top Tip 3 – Stop rushing around

One of the things I tell my ladies is to slow down, just a bit. Take a slightly slower pace. Rushing is a common trigger for hot flushes. Next time you are out food shopping, just stand still for a moment and watch all the women rushing around the supermarket and then notice all the red necks and faces.

It's not about going at a snail's pace, just a better one for you. There is such a thing as 'Rushing woman syndrome.' An article about it appeared in a national newspaper, commenting on how it was a trigger for hot flushes. Just what I've been saying to my female clients. It is good to have my thoughts and beliefs confirmed, if you like, by someone in the medical profession, even if they are not aware of it.

Getting flustered, for some, again is a trigger for a hot flush. Just breathe it out. Use the breathing exercise described in Chapter 1. It is best to practise it every day so that it becomes your automatic reaction to stress, anxiety, worry, any uncomfortable feelings or emotions. You may find that just realising that you are feeling flustered or rushing is enough.

Top Tip 4 – Tweaks to your lifestyle

As I have said before, menopause is about making tweaks to your lifestyle, adjustments.

So, what do you need to tweak? Not sure? Ask yourself these questions –

1. Do you have a stressful job?
2. Is your personal life stressful?
3. Are you under a lot of pressure to perform, meet tough deadlines, long working hours or want/need to be perfect?

If you answered yes to any of these three questions, my recommendation is to start using the breathing technique mentioned in Chapter 1. What can you change in your working life? When is enough, enough? Where are you going to draw the line, the boundary between work and personal life? As you step out of the door at work, mentally leave work at the door. Whatever you wear or carry on you that represents work, e.g. lanyards, keys etc. take them off as you get to the door. This will send that message to the brain that work is done. Use the journey home to calm down and switch to home mode.

Personal life can be a little trickier. What is stressful at home? What can you control? Look after yourself, take time out for you, smile and laugh with those you love. Ask for help from those around you.

4. Do you feel anxious?
5. Are you having panic attacks?

Use the breathing as mentioned before. Acknowledge the feeling, then tell yourself you will be okay. Imagine yourself feeling calm and comfortable, at ease.

If you answered yes to any of the above, you may well benefit from private sessions with a hypnotherapist or a counsellor. In my experience, these conditions usually respond really well to hypnosis.

6. Do you eat three meals a day?
7. Do you eat fresh fruit and vegetables?

Make sure your meals include those foods that contain vitamins and minerals that will support you through the menopause. Healthy nutritious food in, means more energy out, fewer menopause symptoms, better performance, clearer skin and feeling much better generally. See food charts in Chapter 4.

8. No time to exercise?

Be more active. Exercise does not have to mean going to the gym unless you enjoy it. You can be active, have fun and spend time with your loved ones just through gathering together, playing games with the children. Find excuses to move around more like using stairs instead of lifts.

Have Fun.

Top Tip 5 – Your attitude to all of this!

Your attitude to menopause is key. As I have mentioned before, the way we think physically affects the body. It also affects our feelings and the way we view the world or our world.

Feeling down and negative about this phase will make your symptoms worse. Even the brightest of days will seem duller. Yes, you are right, there are days when we will feel naturally a bit lower in mood, everyone does. But, it's how you handle that feeling that makes the difference. You have a choice, sit back and wallow in feeling down. Notice that you then sink even further into it and it also lasts a whole lot longer. Or, you can say to yourself,

'Yes, I feel a bit low today, so I'm going to go and do something.'

Take your mind off it. Go for a walk, have a cuppa with a friend anything that is not dwelling on the feeling. Notice, how much better you feel in a short space of time, that the low mood has not lasted long. The question is:

'Which course of action do you want to take?'

Through being, thinking and acting positively life will be so much better. Your quality of life will be the best that it can. Your experiences and interactions with people and the world will be far superior. You are helping your body to work as well as it can.

Just to show you the mind-body connection this is the exercise in Chapter 8 again for you to try.

- Find a partner.
- Put your arms out in front of you, a bit like a zombie pose!
- Then the partner just presses down gently on your arms to show your normal resistance
- Next, still with your arms outstretched, think of the absolute worst thing that has ever happened or could happen to you. In other words, think negatively.
- Again, get your partner to press down on your arms. You should notice that they are easier to push down. Less resistance.
- Finally, repeat the exercise, but thinking about the best, most awesome thing that has ever happened or could happen to you.
- Lastly, get your partner to press down on your arms. You should notice that there is more resistance. Not so easy to push down.

Swap over and repeat the whole exercise with your partner. You are pushing down on their arms.

Hopefully, this will have shown you the effect of thinking, being and acting negatively upon your body. Even on my darkest day, when I said goodbye to my mum, I still remember finding a positive. Looking out of the window, I was grateful for such a beautiful sunrise. You can find something good in every day. You may have to look a little harder sometimes, but you can still find it.

Top Tip 6 – A new you! This is YOUR life

There's a phase in life, when women have children, that they can feel lost. That they have lost who they are. Sometimes feeling like just mum or Melissa's mum, not Sue a person in her own right.

For some women this can happen with the menopause, they lose that sense of self, who they are. You may feel lost but what is lost can be found. Menopause is a time of discovery, a time to get to know a new you. To find that new identity.

For a great many ladies, the past has been about looking after everyone else, meeting their needs, often at their own sacrifice in some way. So, now is YOUR TIME, a time when those around you are more independent and don't need you in the same way. Although, I do acknowledge that for some it maybe elderly parents that require care and help. Even so, it is still your time. Focus on you.

- What do you want to do?
- Who do you want to become?
- How do you want to feel?

Work now on what you want your future to be like, feel like and who you want to be. If you want to be one of those sprightly, fit and sharp as a knife, wise old women, then you need to work on it now. Go to an exercise class that you enjoy, that makes you laugh while huffing and puffing. Engage in conversations with people, be an active member of your family and the community. Belong to a group. Do new things and go on adventures. Don't let excuses get in your way. There is usually a solution to the problem, you just need to find it. Have fun. Enjoy life as much as you possibly can.

Be the best version of you that you can possibly be. Embrace the sense of freedom and liberation that comes with menopause.

Top Tip 7 – Support from your network and friends or me

This may sound simple, but you would be surprised how many women suffer in silence. There is growing recognition that some ladies need support in the workplace while going through the menopause. However, I do think that much more recognition and understanding is required in this area by those in positions of authority.

It is essential that we enlist support from those around us. Sometimes, just that understanding from others can make a world of difference. This is a great example, a friend attended a networking meeting, which consisted heavily of men in an enclosed room. When she was getting hot (before we started working together), she would open one of the big windows to let in cool air, even in the depths of winter. The men would be shivering and freezing but said nothing as they knew once she cooled down she would shut the windows. A perfect example of understanding, tolerance, patience and compassion.

Just letting others that you spend a lot of time with know how this is affecting you, what you are going through can make a big difference. Once they are aware, you will find, that they begin to recognise the signs that you need help and intervene.

You can also gain support from me. I have a Facebook page, Pebbles Hypnotherapy or you are welcome to email me through the contact form on my website. In addition to that, I work privately with individual clients, so everything is specific to them. If you would like to know more about this contact me through my website www.helenbreward.com OR email me at helen@helenbreward.com

Top Tip 8 – Being kind to yourself

Speak kindly to yourself. It's easy to be negative and that inner critic. A rule of thumb, if you wouldn't say it to a child, then don't say it to yourself.

Be your own gatekeeper, replace those negative thoughts with a positive one as soon as possible. The more you do this, the less you will need to do it. You are essentially training your brain to be more positive.

Start each day with a smile and saying something nice to yourself.

You are amazing.

End each day thinking about all the positive things from the day, no matter how small they are. Sometimes, just getting to the end of the day is a massive achievement in itself.

Today I was awesome.

Top Tip 9 – Forget about it

It is a known fact that you get what you focus on. So, think about what you actually want, how you want to feel, rather than what you don't want.

How many times have you focused on hot flushes, to be rewarded for your thoughts and efforts? Again, more proof that your mind is extremely powerful. With that in mind, imagine how good it is to feel cool; how great you feel. Forget to remember about those hot flushes. Remember to forget about those tropical moments.

Let's try an experiment.

Spend the next week focusing and thinking about how cool and calm you feel. After seven days email me and let me know what happened – helen@helenbreward.com

Top Tip 10 – What's good for you?

Sometimes we must do what is best for us, but we can also feel guilty about it. My personal belief is that what is good for us will ultimately be good for those around us in the end.

This is a time for you to start putting yourself first, looking after you. Do something fun, learn something new, relax and enjoy life.

Your 3 Step Action Plan

Now that you have read the book

My 3 step Plan of Action, now that I have read the book.

1. What are your symptoms?

Use the space below to jot down your symptoms. If you are having hot flushes make a note of how many on average, you are having in the daytime i.e. before you go to bed. Then note down how many you have during the night when you are in bed.

2. Identify your triggers.

It may be useful here to refer to the list of common triggers in the Top 10 Tips section. The aim is for you to be aware of food, drink, situations and circumstances that set off symptoms or make them worse. Use the space below to note anything that could be a trigger and the reaction you had e.g. a glass of wine – massive hot flush in the night.

3. Take action.

Now you are more aware of your symptoms and their triggers, you are better able to do something about them. Below is the start of a list of actions you can take next with space to add your own.

a) Download the free hypnosis recording and listen to it every day. www.helenbreward.com/menopause-my-way

b) Cut out those foods and drinks that definitely set me off.

c) Find alternatives to the above food and drink that do not adversely affect me.

d) Checking the food charts, make sure I include as many as I can into my diet.

e) Become more physically active i.e. exercise class, swimming, walking etc.

f) Do something just for me regularly, every day, every week.

g) Seek support from family, friends or from. www.helenbreward.com/contact

h) Say something positive to myself every day

i) Have fun, smile and laugh

Now you have completed these 3 steps enjoy your life. If you would like to work with me on an individual basis, or through Skype, please contact me through my website www.helenbreward.com/contact or helen@helenbreward.com

If you would like to work with one of my practitioners go to www.helenbreward.com/find-a-practitioner

Have an Awesome Life

because

You are Awesome

Printed in Great Britain
by Amazon

64660213R00088